# THE
# CLOCKMAKER'S
# BOX

*Collected Forewords and Afterwords*

## TAHIR SHAH

# THE
# CLOCKMAKER'S
# BOX

*Collected Forewords and Afterwords*

# TAHIR SHAH

MMXX

Secretum Mundi Publishing Ltd
Kemp House
City Road
London
EC1V 2NX
United Kingdom

www.secretum-mundi.com
info@secretum-mundi.com

First published by Secretum Mundi Publishing Ltd, 2020
VERSION 08102020

THE CLOCKMAKER'S BOX

© TAHIR SHAH

Visit the author's website at:

Tahirshah.com

ISBN 978-1-912383-65-8

# CONTENTS

# INTRODUCTION

ONCE UPON A time there was a clockmaker whose clocks were regarded as the most beautiful mechanical objects ever created.

Adorned with fine tracery and exquisite detail, the clocks were extremely expensive to make. The only person in the kingdom who could afford to purchase them was the monarch. With an eye for excellence, and the funds to pay for it, he regularly ordered the clocks, which he presented to other kings.

Whenever one of the clocks was finished, the clockmaker would deliver it to the palace himself, displaying it on a simple silken cushion.

One day, the king, who had commissioned an especially splendid clock, sent word to the clockmaker, asking him to make a presentation box worthy of the timepiece. Following orders, the master craftsman fashioned a rather plain leather-bound box, in which the clock was presented to a visiting monarch.

The next time the king ordered one of the clocks, he asked that the box be a little more ornate – reflecting the sumptuous object it contained.

Time passed.

Each year, the king ordered more and more of the clocks. Utterly obsessed with them, he befriended other sovereigns merely so that he could present them with one of the marvellous mechanical objects.

Each time he placed an order, the king asked that the container be a little more ornate than the time before. Following instructions, the clockmaker added extra layers of golden filigree, finer grade leather, and lavish details that cost a small fortune.

With every order placed, the boxes became all the more magnificent, although the clocks themselves stayed very much the same.

By now, the boxes were so extraordinarily sublime that everyone followed the monarch's example, and became preoccupied with the containers rather than the mechanisms inside. The reversal of sense was so complete that the clockmaker himself was referred to as 'the box-maker'. Fearful at being singled out for expressing his opinion, the monarch's chief adviser held his tongue – even though it was obvious the sovereign was confusing contents with container.

When the king eventually passed on to the happy hunting grounds, a tremendous mausoleum was prepared, decorated with details from the legendary boxes the master craftsman had made. A special slab of marble was mined, and the king's long appellation and many titles were inscribed in lovely lettering upon it.

Beneath them, in pride of place, were etched the words:

KING, RULER,
LOVER OF BOXES

The reason I mention this story is because even a humble author is at times in danger of behaving, or rather *misbehaving*, like a king.

Just as the sovereign encased the clocks in boxes of astonishing delight, a writer risks falling prey to suffocating their work with introductions, prefaces, and afterwords.

I wrote the texts presented in this book as a way of complementing my own corpus, and in some cases the writing of others, so as to draw attention to certain themes and ideas, allowing the reader to observe the material in a different way.

When I had finished my first travel book, my father – the writer and thinker, Idries Shah – reviewed the manuscript. Having suggested I change the book's title, he urged me to delete the extensive introduction.

I asked him why.

'Because no one reads introductions,' he said.

'Why not?'

'Because they always think they'll be boring beyond belief.'

To anyone who happens to find *The Clockmaker's Box* in their hands, I offer apologies and thanks...

Apologies for boring you senseless, if indeed I do.

And, thanks for supporting my need to release my work how I wish.

Tahir Shah

# A Moroccan Voyage

THE OTHER DAY a man approached me down at the port.

I was waiting for a friend, a friend who is always late. As someone who moved to Casablanca from northern Europe, I find it near impossible to be late myself. Punctuality is quite unfortunately in my blood. So whenever my friend and I arrange a rendezvous, I always spend half an hour or more glancing at my watch, fussing at his tardiness and at my inability to learn from the past.

So I was standing there, a little on edge, and a little irritated at what I imagined to be a waste of time, when a short, stout figure in a tattered *jelaba* staggered towards me. On his cheeks was a week's crop of tattered grey beard, and on his feet were a pair of grimy *baboosh* slippers.

When he was close, his face fifty centimetres from my own, he put down the basket of fish he was carrying, cleared his throat, and began to laugh.

As I had the time to make use of my curiosity, I smiled politely, and enquired what the man found so amusing. He didn't answer at first. He was too busy wiping his eyes. But then, taking his time, he pressed his hands together, palms followed by fingertips.

'To understand the extraordinary,' he said all of a sudden, 'you must learn to appreciate ordinariness.'

I asked what he meant by what seemed to me a random remark. The man touched a calloused finger to his cheek. Then he smiled. It wasn't a big toothy smile, but rather one that was soft, gentle. It filled me with a kind of warmth, as if something unspoken was being passed on. For a split second I thought the first remark was about to be followed by another. But the man's mouth shut tight, and the questionable dentistry vanished. He lifted up his basket by the handle, shooed away a pair of cats that were now sitting before it optimistically, and he strode off towards the old medina.

For an instant I considered going after him. I sensed my weight shifting forward from my back foot. But then, in the moment before stillness became animation, my friend arrived. He spat out an excuse, something about his mother-in-law and a kilo of lamb, and we went for tea.

For an hour, as my friend rambled on about the challenges of his life, and as the waiter circled our table like a tired old shark, I thought about the man with the basket of fish.

I couldn't get him out of my mind.

At length, when our meeting was at an end, my friend and I exchanged pleasantries once again, good wishes for each other's families, and we parted. But I was on auto-pilot, because still, all I could think of was the man and the fish, and what he had said: *To understand the extraordinary, you must learn to appreciate ordinariness.*

I have spent twenty years in search of the extraordinary. I've written books about my quests for it, and have made television documentaries about it too. I have ranted on to anyone prepared to listen about the glorious energy, the sheer intensity of the unusual and the unexpected. I've risked my life in the mountain ranges of Afghanistan, and in the jungles of the Upper Amazon, and have surmounted all sorts of difficulties on the trail of oddities and the bizarre.

Through each of those years, the extraordinary has been my currency, one that I have hoarded and squandered, and enjoyed with every breath. And in all that time, the months and years in celebration of the peculiar, I have never given any thought or time to considering the exquisiteness of the ordinary form. It had always seemed like comparing consommé to goulash, a delicacy unlikely to satisfy the appetite of a starving man.

But the stray remark at the Casablanca port changed my outlook in the most unexpected way. It coaxed me to appreciate a secret underbelly of ordinariness, a layer of existence so profound, that it is extraordinary in itself.

I have come to believe that we receive things when we are ready to receive them. Like seeds falling on arable land, the right conditions must be present for them to germinate and prosper. Our ability to appreciate takes place in very much the same way. We see – really see – when we are ready to, and not a moment before.

What I find so bewitching is the way the world slips you a jewel when it knows you are prepared to recognize it as a jewel. Equally, you could say there are jewels all around us, but ones that will only be activated for our particular perception in days and years to come. And that's the spirit in which I find myself, with regard to Eric Mannaerts's photographs of Morocco.

I encourage you to move slowly through the pages you hold between your hands. Spend as much time as you can on each photo, observing from different angles, questioning what you see. Ration each one. Allow your mind to soak up the scenes of a magical land, a land that is a canvas for an artist's genius. These pictures do not feature the grand monuments, or celebrities, but they are a twilight zone of reality, a perception that is utterly familiar to anyone who has lived in Morocco.

The amusing thing for me is that, these days, glossy style magazines the world over devote acres of space to their fantasy of Morocco. It's a destination that's regarded as wildly exotic, rapturously appealing because it mirrors – or surpasses – our own imagination. But most of the time the media's fantasy doesn't echo the genuine article at all.

To understand this extraordinary kingdom, you must understand the ordinary, and hold it tight to your heart. Three rusty chairs on a terrace by the sea, the shadow of a man moving quickly across warm tarmac, a fragment of graffiti on a mottled old wall: this is Morocco, *real* Morocco, the place those of us who live here yearn for when we are gone.

On my travels I have crisscrossed this country. I have visited desert shrines and mosques, palaces, bazaars and citadels. And in the wake of those journeys, I have regaled my audience with tales of colour and mystery. But I've never told them of the silent moments: endless meals alone with a paperback, beaches naked of footprints, railway platforms in torrential rain. It's those moments these photographs remind me of, because they are so private they are impossible to fully explain. Such subtlety is rewarding beyond words if you can catch it, like a whisper on the wind.

This morning when I went to meet my friend, the one who's always late, I asked him something. I asked him to describe the beauty of his land to a person who had lost the power of their sight.

My friend thought for a long time before answering.

He seemed a little nervous, as if I were asking the impossible. Then he glanced out at the street.

'The real beauty of Morocco,' he said pensively, 'can only be seen from the inside out. Search from the outside in and you will never find the truth or the real beauty.'

This book provides a keyhole into the Morocco that touches my heart, and shows the kingdom I love, from the inside out. The pages bear fragments of reality that all together form a carpet, bejewelled and magical, that has the power to transport us to another world, to the land of our dreams.

From: *Un Voyage Marocain*

# A Son of a Son

THIRTY-THREE YEARS AGO, an elderly friend of my parents invited me to tea at The Travellers Club on Pall Mall.

I knew nothing about him except that he had been an inseparable friend to my grandfather, The Sirdar Ikbal Ali Shah.

As plates of prim sandwiches with their crusts cut off were served, along with pots of orange pekoe tea, we made polite conversation. Doing as my father had trained me to do, I listened three times as much as I spoke. And, whenever given the opportunity to talk about myself, I turned the conversation around, so my host might have an opportunity to tell me about his life.

I learned that during a long and distinguished career the gentleman had worked for the British Foreign Office in various capacities. Now in his eighties, he was at last able to reflect on travels through Asia, Africa, and the Americas.

When I asked for the high point of his professional life, his eyes seemed to glaze over.

'Pursuing your grandfather,' he said dreamily.

'Pursuing him?'

'Oh yes. Pursuing him to the ends of the earth.'

'Don't quite follow you,' I responded.

The elderly gentleman reached for a scone, lathering it with cream and jam.

'I was spying on him,' he said.

'Spying on him *for*...?'

'For the British Crown.'

'But why?'

'Because the top bods in Whitehall assumed he was up to no good.'

'What would have given them that opinion?'

'The fact that he travelled everywhere – from the wilds of Central Asia, down to the southern reaches of Tierra del Fuego... all under the cover of being a writer.'

'That's what he was.'

'*I* know that, and *you* know that, but the paper-pushers of the Foreign Office didn't believe it for a moment. You see the Sirdar knew people at the very highest levels. He was a close confidante of Mustapha Kemal Atatürk of Turkey, and King Ibn Saud, the Prince Aga Khan, Amanullah of Afghanistan, and was even best friends with King Zog of Albania.'

'Was that really so unusual?'

My host took a bite of his scone, washing it down with a gulp of orange pekoe.

'At the time it was.'

'What was your exact brief?' I asked.

'To follow the Sirdar from a discreet distance, and report back on everything.'

'*Everything?*'

'On where he went and who he met, on what books he was reading, and even on what he was writing in his journals.'

'How long did you follow him?'

'Let me think... First there was a prolonged journey through Afghanistan, Persia, Iraq and the Holy Land. Then a long stay in Saudi Arabia and the Sudan, and after that a North African journey, east to west. A year or so later he and your father made the voyage down to Buenos Aires. All in all, I'd say I shadowed him for about eight years off and on.'

'Surely he knew you were there.'

The elderly gentleman smiled retiringly.

'From the first moment of the first day,' he replied.

'*So?*'

'So he allowed me to do my job. And, rather than making it arduous, he made it very easy. In circumstances when he knew I was listening in, he would speak especially clearly. Or, when he was sitting outside a café making notes as was his habit, he would slip inside to wash his hands, leaving his notebook on the table just long enough for me to take a peek.'

My gaze followed a waiter as he crossed the salon, a silver tray laden with tea balanced on an upturned hand.

'There's something I don't quite understand,' I said. 'You see, my father told me that you were his father's closest friend.'

'Oh but I was,' the gentleman shot back fast.

'How could you have been though, if you were spying on him?'

'I am pleased you asked me that. Very pleased indeed. If you would permit me, I will answer with a description of something that happened one night a little south of Samarkand.

'For weeks the Sirdar had blazed a trail through Afghanistan, with me hot on his heels, dressed in local attire. We had crossed the border north of Mazar-i-Sharif – first him, then I at a distance. I was doing my best to monitor him while sending reports back to London whenever possible. As I described, I was sure he was on to me, because he was so accommodating.

'He had put up in a caravanserai at the small Uzbek town of Kitab.'

'Kitab... the Arabic for *book*?'

'Yes, that's right... As I was to learn, he was drawn there by its reputation as being a centre of the sky-searchers, what's now known as astronomers. It was mid-winter and I was frozen to the bone. To make matters worse, my funds had run out, and there was no hope of getting any more until we reached Samarkand. So I was forced to camp in the stables, with nothing to eat, while your grandfather sat in the teahouse beside a roaring fire, with a feast laid out before him.

'I remember watching him through the window, marvelling at the way he engaged with everyone there – regaling them with tales of his journeys. My face was pressed up to the glass, my body shaking with cold, as the snow began falling more heavily.

'I was about to prise myself away and limp back into the stable block, when I heard a voice speak a name, *my* name. The next thing I knew, the Sirdar had invited me inside to the fire, fed me a meal of mutton and rice, and given me his own blanket.'

'Did he know who you were?'

'Oh yes, of course he did. And he was most courteous. He commended me for following the "breadcrumbs" he had left so diligently, and apologized for travelling at such a furious pace. When I was warm and well fed, he made a proposal.'

'What was it?'

'He suggested that we travel together as equals rather than as adversaries.'

'But was that allowed?'

'Strictly speaking it was not, but if Whitehall didn't know, they didn't know. And from that moment we became inseparable friends. We soon found we shared common interests in all sorts of things, from philosophy and folklore, to architecture, literature and phonetics.'

'Didn't the mandarins in Whitehall ever get suspicious?'

My host smiled from the corner of his mouth.

'Apparently not. We continued to travel together for years.'

I enquired about the journey to Latin America just after the War. As I'd hoped, the elderly gentleman's eyes glinted with delight.

'Your father was about your age,' he said. 'As thin as a rake, and intensely studious. Your grandfather took him as his private secretary, while leaving his younger brother at home in Oxford to finish his studies. The Sirdar was on a mission to find a source of halal meat for troops from the Indian Army. As with so many of his projects, it was misunderstood from the start by the Foreign Office. They were certain he was up to no good, which of course he was not.'

'My father loves to go on about Buenos Aires in the late forties,' I chipped in.

'Quite rightly so. It was the most magnificent of cities. The Sirdar, your father and I strolled down the tree-lined streets with our mouths wide open in wonder. We had of course come from the winter of a land torn to shreds by war. Each afternoon we would sit at Café Richmond on Calle Florida and discuss the state of the world.'

'I hardly knew my grandfather,' I said. 'All I remember is the blurred outline of a man sitting in the garden of his home in Tangier, with the scent of orange blossom.'

The elderly gentleman smiled very slowly, as though he were feasting on a memory.

'There was no one else like him,' he said. 'He was sophisticated, but could get on with anyone. At heart he was an Oriental, but was one with an interest in the ways of the Occident. He was devout, but not in an obvious or superficial way. His faith was between him and God, with no one else in between.'

'How was he with my father?'

'Reserved. One might even say he was cruel. But that was the only way he knew to be.'

The gentleman brushed a crumb of cake from his lapel as his mind focused.

'One afternoon at Café Richmond,' he said, 'the Sirdar took something from his pocket and placed it on the table. It was a *tusbi*, a rosary, the kind carried by Sufis. The ninety-nine beads were beautifully fashioned from red amber. Over the years I'd seen glimpses of it, whether it be in Bokhara, Khartoum, or Marrakech. The Sirdar was in an especially reflective mood that day. He said: "Each one of us is a bead on a string, a bead touching the one before and the one after." He touched a bead and said, "That's me." Then pointed to the one beside it, and said "That is you, Idries." Then, in a voice that was so soft as to be almost mute, he said, "And that bead to the left of you, Idries, will be your son.""

'*Me?*'

The elderly gentleman smiled again, pleased he'd made an impact.

'You are yourself,' he told me, 'but at the same time, you are part of a chain of transmission. The chain stretches back to antiquity, and forward as well, far into the future. It's for you to build on the foundations left by others, and to allow others to build upon yours.'

Thanking my host for his stories and his wisdom, I made my excuses. After all, I didn't want to overstay the hospitality.

As I stood up to leave, he touched a hand to my wrist.

'I've got something for you,' he said.

Before I could reply, he tugged an object from his jacket pocket and pressed it into my hand.

An exquisite *tusbi* made from red amber beads.

'I visited the Sirdar on Halloween 1969,' he said. 'Less than a week before he died. You had been taken to him a few days before that. He was thrilled.'

'Thrilled with what?'

'Thrilled to have a grandson… thrilled to have the next bead on the *tusbi*. Looking back, it was as though he had sensed his death was near – although he could surely not have known quite how near it was. Before I left Tangier, he gave me this rosary, and he made me promise I'd give it to you on a quiet afternoon such as this, when you were ready.'

'Ready for what?'

'Ready to start your life as a writer.'

Three days after meeting the elderly gentleman who'd pursued my grandfather and become his greatest friend, I found a listing in the British Library catalogue for a book 'of poetry in prose' called *Eastern Moonbeams*. Launched in Edinburgh in 1918, it was the very first book my grandfather ever published. The British Library had misplaced their copy, so I searched for one...

...for thirty-two years.

Over the years I began to imagine that the edition didn't exist at all. But then, a few months ago, my long quest paid off. Something stirred me in the middle of the night, caused me to flip open my laptop, and to search eBay for the hundred thousandth time. To my amazement, there it was... *Eastern Moonbeams*, priced at £6.99.

Far more than a book, it's a symbol.

A symbol of the point at which a family of oral storytellers changed medium – from spoken words to written script.

The volume is small and rectangular, about the size of a bar of chocolate. Printed on exquisite laid paper, it contains an introduction by the legendary folklorist, Donald Mackenzie. There's none of the rip-roaring bravado found in my grandfather's later books. *Eastern Moonbeams* is a work that tiptoed into the medium rather than taking it by storm.

The publisher was John Orr of Edinburgh, which appears to be so small a house that they released almost no other work at the time. Although romantic and saccharine, the poetry in prose form was elegant. Holding it in my hand, as I have done so often since it first reached me, I have tried to imagine how my grandfather felt on first reading his name on the front.

My inkling is that publishing the little book had been the idea of my Scottish grandmother, Elizabeth MacKenzie. The two had met the year before, at a sale of flags and teacake for the war effort. My grandmother, who later recounted the episode in her lightly fictionalized autobiography *My Khyber Marriage*, was instantly smitten by the dashing young medical student from the wilds of the Hindu Kush.

In the forty-two years of their marriage, my grandmother wrote journalistic pieces and published books. Although a fiercely independent woman, she was resigned to playing the supportive wife she was expected to be. So, hanging back in the shadows, she typed out my grandfather's work, edited it, and allowed him to shine.

Over four decades he churned out more than seventy books, and many hundreds of pieces of journalism published in every conceivable language. An expert on Central Asia and the Middle East, he was a representative at the League of Nations, an emeritus professor, and a confidante to heads of state.

But above all, he was a writer.

Looking at his life and career as I so often do, I see my own life mirrored in his. No surprise of course, because I've been inspired by his love of travel and adventure, and by the desperate need for freedom. He lived by a pair of mantras, passed down to my father, and then on to me.

The first: 'Time spent on reconnaissance is seldom wasted.'

The second: 'Write, write, write, and the doors will open themselves.'

There was never any question that my father would follow in his footsteps as a writer. But, looking at it as I am doing now, I realize it was my aunt, Amina, who was expected to be the budding author. She once told me how, when aged eighteen in the summer of 1937, my grandfather had brought her two packets wrapped in brown paper and string.

The first contained an Underwood typewriter.

In the second was a ream of paper.

'He instructed me to write a book,' she once explained, 'and that if I did, he would get it published. And that's just what happened. I typed away all summer in the garden. As the leaves began to turn I handed him a manuscript of my first collection of tales – *Tiger of the Frontier*.'

The book was launched the next year by Sampson Low, one of my grandfather's publishers. While I'm certain there were enormous expectations made of her, Aunt Amina wrote relatively little else in her long and amazing life. The handful of books she published showed off her bedazzling sense of imagination – the very same we knew from the stories she told us.

My father was far too sensible to have the same gift of imagination. Practical, level-headed, and thoroughly reserved, he weighed situations up with great care before he acted. What he lacked in imagination, he made up in industriousness. I've written elsewhere how the soundtrack to my childhood at Langton House was that of a manual typewriter clattering away like machine-gun fire.

He wrote like a man who'd been told his family would be executed at dawn were he not to complete the job at hand. I used to watch him. It was one of the most extraordinary things I've ever seen. When he typed, his hands weren't those of an ordinary mortal. Rather, they were the hands of a sorcerer. In the rare moments when they weren't bashing the keys, they were flexing and gnashing, as though filled with an unruly lifeblood of their own.

Considering it now, I get the feeling Aunt Amina was expected to be the writer. Five years older than my father, she was a truly gifted storyteller. But, in the same way cooking a meal requires various flavours, being a writer takes the collision of various elements.

In *The Reason to Write* I set down a great many thoughts about writing. One of the central points was that – while almost anyone can knock out a book if they put their mind to it – very few people are what I call 'real' writers.

Looking at my father and grandfather, I can safely say that they were real writers. They both had the fixation and the obsession. But, most of all, they had the intense dedication needed to make it as a wordsmith. From my life of writing books, I've come to regard it as the single most important factor which guarantees success.

Doing the grind.

It's that simple.

Grind away, even when you're half-blind from editing the manuscript, and when your head pounds, and bother to put in that last damn comma even when you know that no one will notice whether it's there… and you deserve to be where you yearn to be.

Again, I've written about my own path on the writing journey in *The Reason to Write*, so no need to expand on it here. What I want to note is that there's something so incredibly satisfying about building on foundations laid down over centuries by members of my family.

I see it as passing on a baton – a baton handed from one generation to the next – first orally, and then in print.

Over a span of more than a century, my grandfather, father, and I have published hundreds of books. We are merely the newest branches of a tree whose roots stretch downward deep into the soil.

Our recent contribution has spanned three generations, and a hundred years. Beginning with *Eastern Moonbeams*, it has encompassed literature, travel, philosophy, psychology, *belles-lettres*, and folklore.

As I sit here, writing books and thinking about the world, every word I type is connected to every word uttered by my father, grandfather, and by the generations who came before us.

In the following pages I have assembled fragments of the combined corpus of a century. My only hope is that it's as much of a joy to read as it has been to assemble.

From: *A Son of a Son*

# *Africa*

MY EARLIEST MEMORIES are of Africa.

I remember sitting on the grass at Villa Calpe, the Tangier home of my grandfather, The Sirdar Ikbal Ali Shah, my nostrils catching the scent of orange blossom for the very first time. I must have been about two and a half years old. The intensity of that smell, matched by the delicious warmth of the sunlight on my skin, was seared into my memory in the most intoxicating way.

I've been extraordinarily blessed to travel throughout the world, learning first-hand about cultures and traditions. As anyone who has travelled knows, each one of the great continents holds magical delights of its own.

As a parent I have brought my children up to shun favourites, but rather to select particular favourites for certain moments or moods.

In the same way, I dislike being asked for my favourite destination. It's the kind of question posed by people who have not had vast swathes of land and sea pass beneath them. Travel in a deep-down way, and you begin to understand that every place, every experience, every person encountered, is valuable in their own way.

Having said that, of all the regions I've known, Africa is different.

Not that it is more beautiful or mesmerizing than any other, but rather it sings to those who find themselves there with an intoxicating and almost primeval rhythm.

I have read a great many books by people from the

Occident who have lived and travelled in Africa. They wax lyrical about the landscapes, the traditions, and the lack of 'modern' conveniences. Such descriptions and depictions of the continent tend to be written from one angle, and one angle alone. Presented by Western writers, for a Western audience, they lack depth, and rarely reflect the mass of intertwined layers.

Africa is like a wise old grandmother sitting beneath the tree in the shade. Her face is wrinkled, her memory an endless stream of events and stories from long ago. A rollercoaster of experience, her memories are packed with adventures and wonder. As beautiful outside as in, she's inspired by what she's known and seen, and doesn't need to impress anyone because she is who she is.

As the world careens forward at breakneck speed – raging about the latest inventions, electronic sensations, miracle cures, and all the rest – it forgets Africa. One day – perhaps tomorrow, but probably not – people in the Occidental world will wake up and understand that the mighty landmass that stretches south from Tangier to the Cape is humanity's singular and communal manifestation of hope.

By then the natural world may have been decimated, the tribes robbed of their last proud traditions, and the majestic landscapes plundered for the minerals that lie beneath them.

Each night before I sleep, I whisper a silent prayer.

A prayer that the world will wake up and witness Africa for what it is:

A complex crucible of peoples, nature, and awe-inspiring vistas...

A land that can teach us, if we stop robbing it and start listening to the wisdom it is ready and waiting to give.

From: *Africa: The Anthologies*

BREAKING IN AS a travel writer is virtually impossible these days.

No publisher worth their salt will take an unsolicited manuscript, and getting a commission is almost out of the question if you haven't been published before. It's the *crème de la crème* of vicious circles.

The standard way to get a foot in the door is by getting an agent and relying on them to sweet-talk the publisher into taking you on.

But getting an agent is no easy task in itself.

I wrote *Beyond the Devil's Teeth* when I was twenty-three. I had no agent, no publisher, but I did have a raging enthusiasm to produce a book from adventures in India, Africa and South America.

I had been obsessed by the theme of Gondwanaland and by the Indian tribe of the Gonds, and had written a book based loosely on these themes.

The problem was that once I'd finished the book, no publisher would take it. I sent the manuscript to dozens of publishing houses – great and small – and received the standard letters of refusal.

Undeterred, I tried getting an agent.

There was still no luck. I was turned down by absolutely everyone, and became very depressed. I thought the book would never get in print, and I put it on a shelf for three years.

Then, one morning, a friend gave me an idea.

He suggested I get a letter-heading printed, a fabulous one, with many colours and expensive-looking type. It announced the services of a media agency, under the direction of a fictitious chief agent, Mr. William G. Watkins.

Then I sent the manuscript to as many famous people I could think of, including former US presidents, heads of companies, illustrious explorers and corporate visionaries. A small percentage of them wrote back with very good quotes for use in publicity. I printed these on large sheets of brown wrapping paper, wrapped manuscripts of *Beyond the Devil's Teeth* inside, and sent them out again from my own literary agency – Worldwide Media.

Then I waited.

Days passed.

Then a week or two.

I was about to give up hope when, one afternoon, I was sitting in my studio flat in north London eating Campbell's soup from a can, wondering how I would ever make enough money to travel again, when the telephone rang.

I picked up the receiver.

It was a big publisher calling from the top floor of a tall steel and glass building in the West End. A publisher had never called me before. The woman at the other end asked to be put through to William Watkins, the chief agent. She obviously took me for a receptionist.

Thinking as fast as I could, I asked the lady to hold on while I put her through. Realizing that an important chief agent would never be instantly available, I laid the receiver on a chair and took the time to finish my cold soup.

After three or four minutes I picked it up, cleared my throat, and replied in the silky-smooth obsequious voice I assumed my fictitious Mr. Watkins would have.

Yes, I confirmed, I was the agent for the up and coming genius Tahir Shah and, yes, *Beyond the Devil's Teeth* was still available, although I said, lying, the work had sparked considerable interest in the literary establishment – in Britain and abroad.

The woman, a commissioning editor, said she very much wanted to meet Tahir Shah. She asked if I could find out when he was available.

'He is always available,' I said quickly.

'Are you sure?' she replied.

'Quite certain.'

'*Always?*'

'Always!'

'But don't you need to check with him?'

'I just have,' I said coldly.

We made an appointment for the next afternoon. Before hanging up, the editor said that, as the agent, I was quite free to come along to the meeting as well.

'Madam,' I retorted, 'how very kind, but it may be rather difficult for me to attend as well as Mr. Shah.'

More than thirty years have passed since I wrote *Beyond the Devil's Teeth*.

Looking back at the version of myself that made the journeys, I'm captivated by my overpowering sense of enthusiasm. It's a quality that's stayed with me, and has acted as a lens through which I've viewed the world almost every day of my life.

I recently described the process of writing *Devil's Teeth* in a book I published, called *The Reason to Write*. In that work, I detailed the process of feeling my way forward through the unfamiliar writing realm. I didn't have any experience, and most of those around me were certain I'd fail.

But I had enthusiasm – the single most important ingredient for success in any venture. So, as friends and members of my family shook their heads in condemnation, I typed...

And I typed...

Before I knew it, the manuscript was done. I remember thinking that the work was done and dusted – which of course it was not. In many ways, the hard grind had just begun...

The grind of editing the manuscript and, equally important, of hawking it to a publisher, as I've just described.

The thing that interests me now, though, is how the book is a kind of time capsule.

It's a time capsule of a world in which revolution was about to take place. Days after I wrote the final sentence, the Berlin Wall crumbled, and the slate of history was wiped clean.

Equally, it's a time capsule of my earlier self.

Reading the text now, I have been at times desperate to rework it from beginning to end. But I've resisted more than a few necessary tweaks.

In places, the grammar is a groaning mess, and the

descriptions are the reflection of a young man who was trying too hard.

When people tell me they're reading *Beyond the Devil's Teeth*, I sometimes shudder, then launch into apologies for the book's failings.

This was the case last week, when an ebullient New Yorker rushed up after recognizing me at an airport.

Thanking him, I apologized, and suggested he read one of my more recent works instead.

'I *love* that book,' he told me, his eyes wide with sincerity.

'To tell you the truth, it embarrasses me,' I told him.

The New Yorker took a step forward, until he was uncomfortably close.

Extending a forefinger, he poked me in the chest.

'Reading a book is like looking at yourself in the mirror,' he said.

'Not sure I know what you mean.'

'When you look at yourself in the mirror,' he explained, 'you see a version of yourself that no one else ever sees.'

'*So*?'

'So writers are the same with their books. When they read their own work, they're too close to it.'

'And that's a *bad* thing?'

The New Yorker's face seemed to flush.

'You better believe it!' he yelled.

From: *Beyond the Devil's Teeth*

MY EARLIEST MEMORIES are tinged with the scent of Moroccan cuisine.

I was born in England and subjected to a childhood of grey school uniforms, even greyer skies, and to food so bland that it tasted of almost nothing at all. But, unlike my friends in the playground, I was certain the real world was out there – somewhere. It was a fantasy, a Promised Land, a realm of rich textures and dazzling light, a place where the air was fragrant with spices, and the kitchens abundant with the most magical ingredients.

This secret knowledge came about because of my family's love affair with Morocco. My first journeys there were made as a small child in the early seventies – a time when the kingdom was awash with stoned-out hippies, tie-dye and bongo drums, VW Combis, and Rolling Stones songs. I didn't quite understand how a place could be so different from the world in which I lived. It was so utterly mesmerizing, vibrant, and so culturally colourful.

I can remember the pungent, intoxicating scent of orange blossom on Tangier's rue de la Plage, and the taste of summer melons in Marrakech. My tongue still tingles at the thought of the warm almond pastry passed to me one balmy September afternoon in Chefchaouen. And, as for my first sugar-sprinkled pastilla – it stole my heart.

Then decades passed.

My feet traipsed through forgotten corners of the world, but never found their way back to my first true love

– Morocco. Sometimes on my journeys I would close my eyes and be transported back – to the windswept sea wall of Essaouira, or to Marrakech's J'ma al Fna square, or to the twisting, labyrinthine streets of medieval Fès. With eyes closed as if in a dream, I would breathe in deep and sigh, feasting on the smells and the memories.

Then, one morning, living in an East End flat no bigger than a postage stamp, I had a Eureka! moment. It was so obvious. We would embrace the land of my fantasy: we'd go and live in Morocco.

And we did.

It was like stepping through a keyhole into a world touched by a magician's wand. In the years we have lived here, we have glimpsed an unbroken circle of life that's been eroded and disjointed elsewhere. It's a world dominated by values – by chivalry and honesty, by charity and, above all, by a sense of family.

And at the same time, it's a world dominated by food.

Anyone who has ever spent time in Morocco has been charmed from the first meal by the kingdom's astonishing range of cuisine. Through succulent flavours, textures, ingredients, and sheer artistry – they go together, forming an ancient alchemy all of their own.

One of the first things I learned while living here is that most Moroccans prefer eating their own cuisine at home. A meal, especially one prepared for guests, is a sumptuous blend of hospitality and abundance, and is about honouring the invited as much as it is about feeding them. The dishes presented tend to be enjoyed communally, eaten from a central platter or tagine. And, of course, each home has its own carefully guarded recipes, passed on through centuries from mother to daughter.

Like most of my Moroccan friends, I too am sometimes reluctant to eat in restaurants. As with them, I know that what we have at home is superior to almost anything found outside.

But there are exceptions.

When I first heard that an Englishman had given up a promising culinary career in London's West End, swapping it for the Fès medina – where he planned to start afresh – I rolled my eyes. Then I put my head in my hands. It sounded like a recipe for catastrophe.

But, stepping across the threshold of Café Clock, I was utterly enthralled. Not only was its founder, Mike Richardson, a man of magnetic charm, but he had conjured a spellbinding ambience in the heart of a city I hold so dear.

And, as for the food... it's the exception to the rule. At last there is a restaurant that equals the cuisine found in Moroccan homes.

Café Clock's success lies in the subtle flavours of a culinary tradition which itself stands at a crossroads of geography and culture. It's made possible by seasonal foods, by spices, and by raw ingredients that have found their way to the medieval city through centuries, along the pilgrimage routes. After all, for more than a thousand years, Fès has been connected to the farthest reaches of the Islamic world, to destinations as variant as Seville, Cairo, and Timbuktu, Bokhara, Kabul, and Samarkand.

With time, Café Clock has become far more than a place

to dine well. In the tradition of the ancient caravanserais, once found in every town and city between it and Mecca, and beyond, it's a place where people gather. Some are locals, while many more are travellers, gorging themselves on the intensity of Fès for the first time. Together, they swap stories, talk, listen, laugh, and learn from the endless range of cultural events laid on in the crucible that is Café Clock.

Just as I had been anxious at hearing of an Englishman opening a restaurant in Fès, I had wondered a little anxiously how Café Clock's cookbook might look. Making the shift from the experimental fluidity of a kitchen to the restricted world of the printed page is not easy. It's a realm in which too many talented food writers have failed.

But what strikes me squarely between the eyes is how the author, Tara Stevens, has approached this project. From the outset she's harnessed an astonishing perspicacity, and a clear sense of observation. Through watching, tasting, and above all, through listening, she has brought to this book's pages a rare and comprehensive culinary experience.

At the same time, Tara has explained how and where specific ingredients are sourced, and has clarified the ways in which they are used in the kitchens of Café Clock.

The result is far more than a cookbook. It's a key. Immerse yourself in its pages and, in return, it will unlock a domain that's more usually cloaked in mystery, and quite off limits to the outside world.

Study the pages well, and the ancient alchemy is revealed.

From: *The Café Clock Cookbook*

## Casablanca Blues: The Screenplay

AN ASPIRING MOROCCAN actress from a wealthy family had appeared out of the blue, wining and dining Rachana and me over several months.

In a way that was decidedly Oriental, she charmed me more expertly than I'd been charmed in a very long time. Once we had become friends, she enquired whether I might write a movie in which she would play the starring role. The film could be made without any need for outside funds, she said, as her father would pay for everything.

Even though there was no mention of a writing fee, it sounded like a plan.

Oddly, it came along at the same moment I'd decided to write a novel about Casablanca. The only hitch was that the story I had dreamt up was likely to be prickly for the actress and her family, but I brushed that small point aside.

An image had rooted itself in my mind.

That of an ingenuous fresh-faced American arriving at Casablanca airport at the start of a mid-life crisis.

I could see him clearly.

Dressed in a crumpled old Burberry raincoat and fedora, he was a clone of Humphrey Bogart of Rick's Café Américain.

Each night before I drifted off to sleep, I allowed myself to imagine the adventures of the *Casablanca*-obsessed visitor. Within a week or so I had an entire storyline planned out.

Drilling down into the dark side of Morocco's seething modern metropolis, it exposed the subculture of gangsters, corruption, and vice. The story would be played out against a backdrop of crumbling Art Deco architecture and speakeasies, and would highlight the gaping chasm between Morocco's haves and have-nots.

Rachana and the kids had gone to India for the summer. I had considered going with them, but knew full well I'd have got no writing work done. So, I bought a flight to Buenos Aires, rented an apartment in Palermo Soho, and spent the Argentine winter writing the screenplay of *Casablanca Blues*.

Each day I'd get up early as is my habit, and write for eight hours straight. Then, in the mid-afternoon, I would venture into town and imagine myself in the time my father lived in Buenos Aires just after the War.

My mind was very much focused on Casablanca, but the streets I was discovering were cut from the same Art Deco cloth. Now shrouded in a thick blanket of disarray, every inch of pavement hinted at a magical and magnificent past. Buenos Aires became Casablanca, and Casablanca became Buenos Aires – interchangeable reflections of one another.

As the weeks ground by, I found myself slipping into the movie I was writing, reborn as the earnest foreigner doing his best to understand an unfamiliar realm viewed through fragments.

And, as time passed, I churned out page after page of *Casablanca Blues*.

Writing screenplays is the absolute opposite of creating novels.

Book writing is all about lavishing one's readers with

sumptuous descriptions, and developing a story through a long, dependable text. Screenwriting is a case of less being more. It's the *nouvelle cuisine* of the writing business. Use a single word more than is needed, and you're guilty of the most terrible crime.

Not long before, I'd been brought on to write several drafts of an IMAX movie about Ibn Battutah's fourteenth-century journey to Mecca, and through that had learned the basics of writing for the screen. I'd made the mistake of thinking that screen work was Book Writing Lite, when I ought to have seen it was a different animal altogether.

My friend, the American author Paul Theroux, has written scores of fiction and non-fiction books. He once told me that he'd never undertaken screen work.

I asked why not.

'Because it's something I don't know about,' he said.

It was a good point, one I learnt with *Casablanca Blues*. My script was twice the length it ought to have been, largely because I insisted on developing both the male and female leads to the maximum. In fashioning it, I was a cobbler who was used to making riding boots doing my best to fashion a pair of ballet shoes.

While writing the story, I was influenced by the actress who'd asked for a movie. The tale was infused with her existence – the decadent lifestyle of Morocco's super-rich who have no comprehension of reality. For that reason I'm eternally grateful things panned out in the way – and in the order – that they did.

We spend our lives agonizing why things happen, and

why other things *don't*. I've beaten myself up about it for decades now, and have at last understood a salient point:

Everything in the life of a creative person occurs as it does, and when it does, for a reason. Try to change what's meant to be and you get slammed in the face. Go with the flow – even if you question it – and you're swept downriver on a white-water ride of pre-determined wonder.

As you might have imagined, *Casablanca Blues* didn't go down well with the actress. Three days after sending her the script, she messaged back to say it 'wasn't for her'. Rather than being disappointed, I was thrilled, because I had the material all ready for my first novel.

Shoving the screenplay in a drawer, I didn't show it to anyone again. There wasn't any point. I didn't have an interest in becoming a movie writer, and I had no idea how to go about selling a screenplay.

A decade on I have decided to publish the script for *Casablanca Blues* for three reasons:

First, to show writers who have read my book *The Reason to Write* the way a story develops, and how it can be presented in different forms.

Second, to remind authors that their identity is all the material they have produced – not just the selected pieces championed by their publishers.

Third, that one thing leads to another…

Had I not taken up the actress's unpaid offer to write *Casablanca Blues*, I wouldn't have written the novel based on the same story. I wouldn't have begun along the path of a novelist. Instead, I'd have stayed where a great many of my writer friends are – stuck in a niche, too fearful of their publishers and their own creative worth to reach new horizons.

From: *Casablanca Blues: The Screenplay*

# Ceremony

ANTHROPOLOGISTS ARE ALWAYS trying to work out what defines us as human.

They come up with all kinds of things – from the realization of our own consciousness, to our use of tools, to the way we shape our societies.

My take on it all is that we are human because we rely on ceremony and ritual in an almost obsessive way.

We can't help ourselves.

Ceremony is as much us as we are it.

Of course some animal species use forms of ceremony and ritual too – a point which interests me greatly. My thinking is that the ceremonies we've developed can be traced back to our ancient, pre-human ancestors.

I've often found myself grasping how rites provide a lens through which we regard a society or culture. They deliver an intense culmination of tradition, forces, and ideas, all drawn neatly together in an intertwined tapestry.

Those who know me, or who have read my work, will recognize that I'm not an admirer of organized religion. I believe it has caused human society to flounder unnecessarily again and again – rather like a train sent down a branch-line, having been misdirected at the points.

Just as I spurn organized religion, I delight in the form of human culture that is manifested through ceremony. A friend in India once called me 'Tahir Shah the Ceremony Nut'. He noted, quite accurately, that if there was a ceremony taking place within a hundred miles, I'd smell it out and feel a deep yearning to experience it. The only way for me to rid myself of the calling is to witness it – or, better still, to take part.

Not all ceremonies have religious connotations. The most intriguing ones of all tend not to be enacted in the name of faith. For me, ceremonies are catalysts. A person who enters into one is affected by it, emerging in a changed state.

Over the years I've regarded specific ceremonies, documenting them in great detail. Sometimes I've observed them from a distance and, at other times, I've played a key part in the proceedings. I've often taken a far more central role than I have described when writing up my experiences for published books. The reason is that, while I am happy to share my involvement, a part of me prefers to keep a kernel of inner experience to myself.

A few years ago I took part in a ceremony in northern India. I prefer not to go into the details of it here.

What I want to note is this:

The day before the ceremony, I was terrified. Not frightened in a passing way. Not even the fear that bathes you when you watch a horror movie. But the kind of fear you get when you imagine you're going to drop dead.

Unable to sleep that night, I went out at dawn for the ceremony, which was about to begin. Spanning many hours, it involved a number of quite extraordinary tribal rituals that challenged me in a profound, psychological way.

Once it was over, the *pundit* came to me. A sensitive, self-effacing man, he could see I'd been gravely affected by the experience.

'You were fearful before it began, weren't you?' he asked.

I admitted that I had been.

'And now?'

'I'm OK now.'

'Then why did you fear?'

'Because I didn't know what was going to take place.'

'Was the ceremony how you imagined it would be?'

'It was terrifying,' I replied. 'Far more than I expected.'

'Were you more frightened during the ceremony or before it?'

'Before it.'

'Why?'

'Because I feared what I didn't know.'

From: *Ceremony: The Anthologies*

# *Childhood*

I THINK OF my childhood more than most people.

The reason is that, the way I see it, the childhood years are a magical realm of delight – or at least they ought to be. A testing zone for ideas, emotions, sentiments, and all kinds of other interrelated components, they allow a lump of dough to be kneaded before it's baked into bread.

I believe we are born into the world with a default psychological setting, one that prepares us in the most perfect way for life. The problem is that Occidental society has reprogrammed itself to phase out the genius of our original calibration.

Through a decade or more of so-called 'education', children sit in class and are taught how to understand the society they will inherit. However well meaning, I believe the conventional educational system doesn't prepare kids – because it's going about it in the wrong way.

When Ariane and Timur were young I fretted a great deal, anxious for them to evade reprogramming, and maintain the default setting of imagination with which they were born.

One evening, as I got them ready for bed, they asked me for a story. In my restless state, I remembered one my father used to tell us – a tale called 'When the Waters were Changed'.

When they were in their pyjamas and tucked into bed, I told them the tale.

This is how it goes...

There was once a land where the water was very sweet,

and where everyone was very happy. The trees were tall, the flowers scented, and the mountain landscapes pristine.

One day, a man who lived in a remote valley had a dream. Through it, he learned that in the coming weeks, the waters of the region would change overnight. The sweet water everyone knew and loved would be swapped for new water. It would look the same and taste the same, but the new water would change the way people would think.

Through his dream the man came to understand that he had to channel the existing water into a reservoir, and drink only from that supply. Without any other instructions, he did as he was bid to do by his dream. Accordingly, he filled a reservoir and made sure he only drank its water. Then, running through the kingdom, he warned others of the impending catastrophe, begging them to do as he had done.

A little time passed. Just as the voice in the dream had described, the waters of the kingdom were magically changed.

The old water was exchanged with new water.

As has been foretold, the new water caused the people to think in a different way. To the man who was drinking the old water – and who kept thinking in the old way – it was a terrible thing. He found that the new thinking was at odds with everything he believed to be right. Everyone thought in the new way because, of course, they were all drinking the new water – all except for him.

As the months passed, people began to regard the man from the remote valley as insane. They couldn't understand it, but they knew he was wrong and they were right. This conclusion was reached because there were more of them than there were of him.

More time passed, and the man who was drinking from his reservoir of old water found himself becoming increasingly isolated. The people down on the plateau shunned him when he ventured there. They became progressively bitter, asserting that he was sick or mad, or both.

One day, the man could stand it no more. He went to the reservoir of old water he'd kept in secrecy, and drained every last drop. Then, anxiously, he moved down to the plateau and lived among the people there – drinking the new water just like they all did.

At first, they continued to spurn him.

But with time, they saw he was quite sane. After that, they'd say to each other that the man had gone mad for a time but had eventually reverted to normality again thanks to the power of prayer.

In the same way that the man in the story tried to hold out, but had no choice but to go with the flow, I see Ariane and Timur – and all the other kids out there – have no alternative but to be like everyone else.

Or do they?

Perhaps, if we recalibrate ourselves little by little, we'll reach a time when there will be no need for recalibration at all – because we will be exactly as we were at the beginning… programmed in a way we were supposed to be, right from the start.

From: *Childhood: The Anthologies*

# City

BY NATURE I am drawn to extremes.

I like searing heat and freezing cold, towering mountains and pancake-flat plateaux, epic stories, and tales no more than a few lines long. I like journeys that take months to complete, and fast, spontaneous trips which shake you from your comfort zone. I love the countryside – rolling landscapes where there's nothing but nature – and I love cities, too.

My notion of a city is rarely one that's prim and proper – the kind you encounter in the refined capitals of Europe. Rather, my idea of a city is a sprawling, seething cornucopia of people, invention, noise, filth, riot and uproar. The kind of place that shakes you to the marrow of your bones, sucking you in, stirring you around hard as you steep in it like sheets of leather in a vat of dye, before spewing you out at a time of its own choosing.

I love cities because I hate them.

In the same way that I have a grotesque and macabre fascination for medical curiosities, I find myself gripped by city life. For me, the allure of a metropolis is all about the layers.

However hard I try I can't ignore detail.

Walk down a street and my mind bombards me with every smell, sound, and sight. It pleads with me to reach out and touch the wall I'm brushing against, or to taste the heaps of fruit for sale on makeshift carts. As I notice it all, I see it together and set apart. I see the old and the new, the soft and the hard, the light, the dark, the wild and the restrained.

The more I suck it in, the more my mind races at the ingenuity and the interaction, and the more of it I want to experience.

Drawn as I am to wonder, it's no surprise that the conurbations of the Indian subcontinent and the Far East offer me special delight. Walk down the pavement in Kolkata, for example, and you are introduced to an all-encompassing hurly burly of life, wit, wisdom, and problem solving.

A few years ago, while doing just that, I came to a ramshackle street-side stall serving tea in tiny earthenware cups. Under an awning stretched out between three upright poles, I noticed a foreigner who looked decidedly out of place. Wide-eyed and appreciative, he seemed to be savouring every moment.

'Bill from Tuscaloosa,' he said, even before I had sat down on one of the broken old stools.

'Tahir from all kinds of places,' I replied.

We shook hands, my mind noting that Bill's grip was muscular and tight.

'Just arrived,' Bill said.

'Looks like you found your feet pretty fast.'

'Certainly have.'

'What brought you to India?'

Bill sneezed hard, and asked for another cup of tea.

'Needed a dose of frenzy,' he replied.

'*Frenzy*? And did you find it?'

'Yup.'

'What kind of frenzy?'

'The kind you can't get on the Travel Channel,' Bill answered fast.

'As in?'

'As in IMAX 3D taste- and smell-o-vision.'

'With full Surround Sound?'

'That's it!' Bill roared. 'You know it!'

'Yes I do. And why Kolkata?'

'Because it's fully loaded, that's why.'

'Not quite with you.'

Bill appeared disappointed, as though I wasn't keeping up.

'Kolkata looks like a city,' he explained. 'It smells like a city, too, and behaves like a city in every way… but it isn't actually a city at all.'

'Really?'

'Yup.'

'Then what is Kolkata if it isn't a city?'

Bill clicked his neck, left-right-left, and sighed.

'It's an onion,' he said.

'How's that?'

'Because of the layers.'

'*Onion* layers?'

Bill from Tuscaloosa gave me a double thumbs up.

'Now you're getting it!' he yelled.

From: *City: The Anthologies*

# Confluence

ONE OF MY earliest memories is of sitting on the ant-infested lawn of a villa in Tangier where my grandfather had lived.

I was six years old. My father's shadow was cool on my face, long and looming in the approaching twilight.

'You must remember something,' he said in a serious way. 'Something important which will shape your life.'

Looking up, I blinked, and hoped it was something funny.

But it wasn't. Instead, as usual, it was about stories. No surprise in that. After all, my father was obsessed with stories.

'Stories can teach us things,' he said. 'Sometimes they're about good and at other times they're about bad. They can feature ogres and princesses, jinns and treasure, unicorns and kings.'

As usual, my attention waned.

Like every other child, I enjoyed hearing stories, but wasn't interested in how they worked.

Leaning down from his chair, my father brushed the ants from my leg.

'What kind of stories do you like best of all?' he asked.

'Dragons!' I cried out in a shrill voice. 'I like dragons, and dinosaurs as well.'

Pinching a hand to his moustache, he thought for a moment, and brushed away the ants again.

'Stories are an instruction manual to the world,' he said. 'They're more important than any of the rubbish they will teach you in school. In some ways they're the only thing that matters.'

With the shadows lengthening, I got off the grass and clambered onto his lap.

'Will you tell me a story, Baba?' I asked.

'About a dragon?'

I nodded.

'A purple dragon, please.'

Leaning back into the cane chair, he began as he always did, with the four words that are in themselves a portal from the world of mortals, into an enchanted realm: *Once upon a time...*

Decades have passed since that late summer evening in Tangier...

Decades in which I have studied at school, travelled, written books, and raised children of my own. My father may have left us more than twenty years ago, but the stories he imparted are still tethered to me, just as they are very much inside the heads of my two children, Ariane and Timur.

In the years since his death, I found myself reflecting on how stories worked, and why they were important. I pondered the science behind them, and watched with great interest as they were told, retold, and received.

When my children were very small, I bought a rambling mansion called 'Dar Khalifa', in the middle of a Casablanca shantytown. Soon after moving in, I was advised that the house was packed from floor to ceiling with legions of evil jinn (known to Hollywood as 'genies'). In many ways, living at Dar Khalifa was like existing within the pages of *A*

*Thousand and One Nights.*

Against this backdrop – a dominion in which fact and fantasy were blurred into a magical canvas of enchanted possibility – I explored Morocco.

Roaming through the kingdom's deserts and mountains, its ancient medinas and along its coastlines, I found myself in a place set apart from the brutal realities of the Occidental world I had left behind.

Exploring Morocco, I began to descend down through the layers, reaching a bedrock – a twilight zone of wonder rarely experienced by foreigners.

I believe that to understand the kingdom as its own people know it, you have to shut out the obvious, and receive it in an inside-out way. A crossroads of culture for centuries, Morocco has been shaped by folklore as much as it has by invaders, technology, or anything else.

Stories are a glorious fabric woven from reality and imagination. Shaping our world, they are the very essence of humanity.

My father believed that certain tales could be found in many cultures – separated by oceans and seas. He would say that the sagas of the Norsemen, or the tales of Celtic folklore, were linked to Oriental treasuries through a kind of cultural lifeblood.

'If you want to know a country,' he once told me, 'don't bother to view its landmarks, but listen to its tales instead.'

*Confluence* bridges culture in the most profound way by holding up a mirror to who we are. It proves that, however different, we are all cut from the same enchanted fabric, and that we are set free by imagination. Far more than a simple book, it is within itself a repository of ancient know-how, just as it is a reflection of this very moment.

On some nights when I cannot sleep, I think back to the ant-infested lawn at my grandfather's villa in Tangier more than half a lifetime ago. I imagine myself sitting there, squirming with expectation, waiting for the tale of a purple dragon.

A tale which began by slipping through the portal conjured from words:

*Once upon a time...*

From: *Confluence*

# Cultural Research

PEOPLE OFTEN SAY the world has become very small.

By that, I assume they're referring to travel and communication. After all, venturing to the most obscure places on the planet – or communicating with them – has been made easy.

A century ago no one would have been heard moaning that it had taken an hour longer than expected to fly from London to Tokyo. Or that you'd been stuck in a tunnel under the English Channel.

Back then, few could have dreamt of a day when racing from London to Berlin for lunch would not only be conceivable, but affordable, too.

Until relatively recently, most societies had little or no interaction with others far away. Indeed, until a couple of centuries ago, almost no one ever ventured beyond the borders of the territories in which they lived.

A few intrepid explorers did reach far-flung lands, of course, and lived to tell the tale to a wide-eyed audience. Bringing with them strange new fabrics, fruit, or exotic spices, they would have wowed those around them.

In our time, in which just about anything and everything is freely available, it's almost impossible to conceive how things must once have been.

Imagine, for instance, that in Georgian England, pineapples were so rare that the well-to-do would rent one for the evening – not to eat, but to merely show off to their friends.

A century ago, the vile onslaught of the Great War led

to the opening up of cultures on a monumental scale – far more than had ever taken place throughout human history. European nations, and the United States, began influencing not only the lands bordering them, but others on the far side of the globe – on a mass scale.

As regions such as the Indian subcontinent, the Middle East, and Africa increased their exposure to the world outside their own borders, there was a direct influence on their societies, and on their ancient cultural systems as well. Newly introduced products and ideas had an irreversible effect – from Buenos Aires to Bangkok.

A profound knock-on effect took place, as the prevailing winds of change tore through great cities, towns, villages, and hamlets. All of a sudden, it was possible to buy a Savile Row suit in Mexico City, Swiss clocks in Vladivostok, or indeed a pineapple in Bradford.

The nineteenth century had been an age in which science, having powered the Industrial Revolution, found itself very much at odds with the Church. At the same time, 'cults' of all kinds were introduced into English society, as discussed by Robert Cecil in his fascinating paper.

Within Britain's Victorian age, all areas of life witnessed monumental change and upheaval. With a plethora of goods and services to supply, its mighty empire sought to recalibrate the world. As it did so, it ended up being transformed as well – influenced by immigrants and their unfamiliar ways of life.

Change ripped across each continent in turn, forcing fragile societies that had been isolated for thousands of years to adapt or to be relegated to extinction – as so many inevitably were.

They say history is written by the victors.

More fundamentally, it's written by those whose cultures endure, rather than be annihilated.

Through the readings in this book, we'll see how certain civilizations have boomed, while others have had their ancient cultural heritage diluted, and destroyed.

The Gond tribe of Central India, for instance, the indigenous Ainu of Japan, and the so-called 'Kafirs' of the Hindu Kush: each was compelled to abandon traditions and beliefs that had evolved through centuries.

The enduring mantra of the time was very much one of 'adapt or die'.

In the northern Japanese island of Hokkaido, the few pure Ainu that remain were forced to abandon antique ways of life – tailored to their individual circumstances. As has taken place with ubiquitous regularity, the new realm decreed that one size and shape of culture fits all.

Similarly, the Gonds of Central India were driven from their lands, destined to become inferior, eking out a living at the margins of society. And, as in the case of some ancient Kafir tribes, they were dispossessed, left with little choice but to sell traditional carvings to tourists.

Parallels can be drawn between such people as the Gonds, the Ainu, and the Kafirs. We will see how each culture was once autonomous, self-reliant, and calibrated to the place where they resided.

Such societies had no need for the world beyond the

frontier, or the trappings of its commercialization. But, as secluded communities fell under the jurisdiction of others, and as bureaucracy developed, they were stripped of their own systems of regulation and control.

The increased interaction between people of different nations leads to complexities on all fronts. With conflict the name of the game, it became necessary to establish legislative systems to preside over cases with foreign elements.

At the same time, enslaved people shipped to the New World in their millions did their best to cling on to indigenous beliefs. These convictions, reflected through faiths, were influenced by fresh environments. The philosophies of First Nations melded with the principles of certain West African secret societies, to create extraordinary new hybrids, such as 'Macumba'.

Dance, music, and other key cultural constituents travelled westwards with the human cargo, forcibly transported to the New World. Having reached their destination, they continued to develop.

Spurred on substantially by the rise in technology, the last century has brought riches to a select few, just as it's robbed many more of their culture, work, and land. Many countries, such as some in the Arab world, benefitted – at least on the surface.

All of a sudden there was a value in the unseen wealth lying beneath the sands they'd roamed for an eternity.

In his inspirational paper on the years that he spent with the Arabs, General Sir John Glubb writes of the simple courtesy and dignity of a people he had known before their lives were brutally changed by technology.

Peter Brent sums up the sense of awe and mystique Arabia still holds for many. Remembering the descriptions of early travellers through Arab lands, he discusses the wave of catastrophic change caused by the modern age – highways slicing through the desert, gridlocked with air-conditioned limousines.

At its height, an Arab Caliphate stretched the width of Africa, and across much of Asia, lasting for centuries. In that time, it produced some of the most magnificent architecture, literature, and art of any civilization.

But every empire comes to an end.

Within Europe, the great Islamic dominion of the so-called 'Golden Age' eventually broke up. The Moors, who had ruled the Iberian Peninsula for more than seven centuries, were defeated. Those not expelled were driven into subservience. Converting on pain of death, these *Moriscos* ('Little Moors') endured. Against extraordinary odds, some even managed to continue their Islamic beliefs in secret, and even produced a considerable body of literature.

Now that communication has become faster and easier, we are informed about cultures from every corner of the earth. But, rather than merely observing them – in books, documentaries, and online – we must learn about them in a deep-down way. By studying their ancient methods, we have a hope of solving the problems we ourselves face.

Our society is riddled with trials and tribulations of all kinds – predicaments and problems that are endemic in all the lands we have influenced and changed.

The papers in *Cultural Research* illustrate a sense and sensibility that we've lost but can and *must* re-learn. Through reading of the experiences of others, we can understand our own society and seek answers, not only to our own problems, but to those of the wider world.

From: *Cultural Research*

# Danger

I OFTEN THINK of the medieval pope who hated cats more than anything else.

He gave an order for every last one to be hunted down and killed. This was done. Cat-lovers wept while, I assume, the Pope danced. In the weeks and months that followed, the lack of cats led to an immediate and startling rise in rats.

And the abundance of rats meant that fleas prospered like never before.

This in turn led to plague...

Black Death, which swept through Europe, killing millions... all because one powerful man loathed cats.

There is of course no way the Pope could have known that exterminating our feline friends might have brought society to the brink of annihilation.

But it did.

In the same way, removing danger from society, or at least reducing it as much as possible, has an effect.

I have noticed this with my own children, Ariane and Timur.

They have been raised with care and attention, in a way that every parent would wish for – which is of course good and right. After all, the last thing any one of us wants is to expose our children to potential harm.

My take on danger is this:

When someone has been protected from danger whenever possible, they don't recognize its shadow. In the same way we must learn how to identify poisonous berries on a bush, we need to appreciate all forms of danger, and know how to recognize them.

This is something I frequently turn over in my mind.

One of the reasons I took Ariane and Timur to live in Casablanca when they were very small was to expose them to a realm in which danger was an ever-present shadow.

In Europe I'd witnessed accidents and tribulations take place, all because endangerment had been eliminated lock, stock, and barrel. In my opinion, Occidental society is becoming weaker because it's coddled and protected.

We live in a time preoccupied with safety – in which nothing is quite so important as eliminating danger.

And, what's wrong with that?

Nothing at all.

Since the beginning of history our ancestors were preoccupied with survival. To survive they had to avoid being swallowed up by wild animals, poisoned, or slain in battle. For them, danger was a well-known abhorrence – one that was never more than an arm's length away.

Peer into the lens a little deeper and it's easy to consider danger differently.

One of a family, its siblings are risk, fear, mayhem, and disaster. None is particularly pleasant, but each one is vital in its own right.

My argument is that by lessening the circumstances in which danger arises, we create a situation in which a hazardous knock-on effect takes place. Change one element in the wider scheme of things, and dominoes begin to fall.

Once in a while during my travels I encounter someone

who personifies an idea that's gripped me for a good long while. Best of all is when I come across the same individual again and again – allowing me to draw wider conclusions.

During the nineties I was a frequent visitor to Istanbul. I was fascinated by the way the city was changing – affected as it was by the recent breakdown of the Soviet Union. All kinds of fantastical characters were washed up there at that time – including a great many Kazakhs, Uzbeks, and Turkmen.

A chance encounter at a café introduced me to the life and ways of a man called 'Sukhan'. A raw, sinewy brute, he hailed from the Turkmen capital, Ashgabat, and had been drawn to Istanbul by the prospect of a great future.

Sukhan and I met because he robbed me. Or, rather, he tried his level best to do so while I was scribbling notes in the winter sun. Lost in my own world, I felt a hand slipping into my jacket pocket with the dexterity of a viper slithering silently into a hole.

In an overly dramatic reaction, I snatched the thieving hand, holding it tighter than tight. Panning up from the knuckles, I found it led to an arm, the arm to a body, the body to a head, and the head to the most charming of faces, dominated by a Charlie Chaplin grin.

'Do you have a cigarette lighter?' the thief asked.

'No, I don't smoke.'

'OK.'

'You were trying to rob me!' I declared heatedly.

'Cigarette lighter. I was searching for cigarette lighter.'

'Well, you could have asked me rather than go through my pockets!'

'You were writing in book. Didn't want to disturb.'

Narrowing my eyes, I regarded the thief with hatred.

'I am Sukhan!' he cried out, as though the name excused his sins.

The next thing I knew, we were sitting together, drinking apple tea, and talking about life. Sukhan revealed how he had come to Istanbul to become a fight club champion in the anything-goes bouts held each night in the Gülsuyu Quarter.

'I like fighting,' he said, the words followed by his signature Charlie Chaplin grin. 'Fighting is good!'

'Do you get injured?'

Sukhan cackled at the question.

'Yes! It's good. Getting injured is good.'

'Is it?'

'Yes!'

'Why?'

'Because getting injured makes muscles grow.'

Having paid my bill, I checked my wallet and my wristwatch, and bade Sukhan the bare-knuckle fighter farewell.

'We will be friends forever,' he said with certainty, as I turned to leave.

I doubted it, but it was a prophecy that seems to have come true.

Over a period of seven or eight years, we would meet at the same table, in the same café, whenever I was in town. I would tell Sukhan about my travels, and he would show off his scars. I was no expert in fight club tactics or rules, but it struck me as though my friend from Ashgabat was getting injured a great deal.

On one occasion he showed off a torn ear. The next he had railway track stitches down his right cheek. Another time, his ribs were bandaged and, at yet another meeting, he grinned with delight at having sustained a broken ankle.

'Why don't you stop this madness and get a job?' I begged one late spring afternoon.

'Because I like fighting!' Sukhan grinned. 'Fighting makes me happy.'

'But how?!'

The Turkmen from Ashgabat ran a fingertip down the train track stitches on his face.

'Because life with danger is good life!' he said.

From: *Danger: The Anthologies*

# *East*

HAVE YOU EVER reflected on how something can mean totally different things to different people?

I have.

It's something I dwell on a lot of the time, turning over in my mind how a certain person will grasp hold of a definition which, to me, seems utterly misguided and wrong. Of course, there's every possibility that someone else is right and that it's me who's wrong. But the way I see it, one of the great joys of life is experiencing something that changes your definitions, prejudices, and perceptions.

All of this comes into play, as I sit here at my desk, reflecting on the word 'East'. It's arbitrary of course, because there's no such thing as East or West, North or South, up or down. It's a label meted out centuries ago by crusty old colonials in Europe to delineate a region fit for plunder.

For me, the word 'East' is loaded with connotation, a word representing two distinct streams of emotion and thought.

My father was half Afghan and half Scottish, and my mother was half Parsi Indian and half English. Throughout my childhood we were based in England, although we frequently travelled to Morocco and Europe. Never once did we go to the 'East' – east of Europe, that is.

In place of actual travels, my father would fill the void with a dream-like extravaganza of information – most of it presented as stories. We learnt of the East in a way that had little bearing on the actual place, but in a way that fulfilled my father's own needs.

As far as he was concerned, his children had to know where they had come from as per the Oriental method – not through an A to Z appreciation, but rather in fits and bursts, layer upon layer, in a way that seemed dangerously random.

The result was that I imagined I knew the East long before my feet ever reached it. I knew how it smelled and sounded, what the people were like, how the sun felt on my skin, how the mountain ranges looked in winter, and all the rest. My interpretation was of course a fragmentary and bizarre fabrication of what actually existed.

Rather like a child who'd never seen a magnificent ocean liner, but had it described to them, I'd built up a picture, laid detail upon detail – through sight, smell, taste, touch – but most of all through the words of stories.

So, when I finally arrived in the so-called 'East', it was a considerable shock.

The version of Eastern reality presented to me through a prolonged childhood was certainly a skewed representation of reality. As I soon found for myself, the genuine article is far more glorious than something understood by observing reflections.

Since my teens I've crisscrossed landscapes that my father regarded as the 'Oriental'. He tended to use the word in the widest possible fashion, infusing it with an ancient methodology and know-how.

The extraordinary thing about having known the East in an inside-out and upside-down kind of way – before I knew it in reality – was that I found myself perceiving patterns invisible to those not primed the way I had been.

Through the alchemy of my childhood, I was prepared to pick out threads of culture and behaviour, beauty, emotion, and horror, invisible to others from the Occident.

A life of travel has taught me not to presume to be an expert, but rather to be a consummate admirer. Seeing visitors from Europe or elsewhere traipsing through Eastern lands, railing with rage at what they regard as shortcomings, saddens me. I'm terribly impatient with impatient people. I can't bear moaners and groaners. Instead, I delight in those who can see magic levels that everyone else has missed. The Oriental realm is awash with layers and details galore.

Four years ago, I visited Myanmar with Ariane and Timur. I was delighted to have been granted a visa as, only a year before that, I'd been firmly refused.

One morning we visited a particular shrine at Bagan. Through its long history, pilgrims had visited it in the hope of having their prayers answered. On the day we arrived, it was inundated with tourists from Russia. Hundreds and hundreds of them, they'd turned up in a huge group. Posing for selfies, they didn't appear to be taking in the awe-inspiring beauty of the place.

Fortunately, they surged away as quickly as they'd come, leaving us alone at the shrine. When they were gone, we spent time in silence taking in the layers of life and history.

As I paced around the shrine, my attention was drawn to a certain marble stone on which a handprint had been sculpted in counter-relief. Observing it, I marvelled at the genius of the artist who'd created such a lovely thing. It was so subtle one hardly realized it was there.

Ariane found me caressing the stone with my own hand.

She pointed out that it wasn't sculpted but rather it had been created over centuries. Every time a pilgrim passed that spot, they would touch the stone to steady themselves, as the ground beneath it was uneven.

'If the ground was flat that stone wouldn't have ever been touched,' Ariane said.

'Thank God the ground is uneven,' I replied. 'And that the builders of the shrine were too lazy to chip away at that chunk of rock at ankle-height.'

Ariane slipped me a sideways smile.

'What if the builders left the rock down here on the ground,' she replied, 'knowing that over centuries people would have to touch the stone as they passed?'

'That's forward thinking.'

'It's more than that,' Ariane said. 'It's thinking inside out.'

From: *East: The Anthologies*

## Expedition

As a small child at Langton House, I had a battered old cardboard box in the corner of my bedroom.

On each side was a picture of two giant upright bananas, a hammock slung low between them, along with a caption: 'Welcome to Bananaland!'

The box arrived when I was about six, and was still there in the corner of my bedroom when Langton House was sold seventeen years later. In that time, it got more and more bashed about, but was much prized for what it contained.

*Expedition equipment.*

I'm not sure if it was the banana box that first sowed the idea of exploration, or whether it was the precious objects inside that stirred me. I like to think it was a mixture of the two.

For as long as I can remember, the banana box was a receptacle for the kind of gear I imagined would be needed on a grand expedition. As I'd never been on an expedition, I relied on *The 1971 Scout Annual* and word-of-mouth information passed on by the full gamut of characters who visited us.

Whenever an elderly gentleman strode through into the hallway, I'd slink out of the shadows and ask if they had been on an expedition. Sometimes they responded politely that they had not, or that they had but it was too long ago to remember the details. But not infrequently, they would clap their hands together as if having won the Derby, and reveal everything they knew.

One of the most reliable elderly gentlemen who came to Langton House was a military man called Dr. Grimes. No matter the weather, he was invariably dressed impeccably in tweed, a farmer's checked shirt, and a regimental tie. Langton House seemed to instil politeness from its visitors, but Dr. Grimes took courtesy to an entirely new level.

Looking back, I sense he had absolutely no interest in discussing expeditions with a six-year-old but, such was his expertise, he gave the impression that nothing on earth would give him greater pleasure.

Before Dr. Grimes would visit, I would ask my parents over and over if he was a true expert on the expedition business.

'Of course he is!' my father would exclaim.

'No one's done more expeditions than Grimes,' my mother would add, looking up from her knitting.

'What kind of expeditions does he know about?'

The question would cause both my parents to appear transfixed, as though they had seen angels.

'He's done them all,' my father would say.

'Searched for treasure?'

'Oh, yes, of course.'

'Lost cities?'

'So many, yes!'

'Unknown animals?'

Again, my father would nod frantically.

'Another one of his specialties.'

'Do you think Dr. Grimes minds me talking to him?' I would ask.

'I think he likes it very much,' my mother would say.

'Why?'

'Because I suspect it reminds him of his youth.'

Over the years Dr. Grimes visited, he would ask how my equipment was getting on, and would ask to see any new bits and pieces I had sequestered away in the banana box.

Sometimes I'd show him a few feet of parachute cord I'd found on the ground in the village, or a clutch of bottle caps pressed from a sheet of extra-thick tin.

'Very useful,' Dr. Grimes would intone. 'This will be just what you need when you're on the expedition.'

One day, when Dr. Grimes and I had got to know each other better, I hurried over as soon as he'd blustered in through the hallway.

'I think it's time you start planning some expeditions,' he said.

'*Some expeditions?*'

'Yes.'

'Don't you think I ought to begin with one expedition and see how that goes?' I asked anxiously – after all, I was only eight.

'Oh no… no, no, no,' Dr. Grimes responded fast. 'You must always plan several expeditions at once.'

'Why?'

'Because it's the only way to be certain of thinking big!'

'How big should I be thinking?' I probed warily.

Dr. Grimes beckoned me forward. By this point he was sitting in a low armchair in the drawing room, his face in line with my own.

Stepping forward, I observed him, my mind mapping the wrinkles, the broken veins, and the individual strands of silvery bristle that formed his moustache.

His bloodshot blue eyes peering deep into mine, he responded:

'When you're older you will find something to be true.'

'What, Dr. Grimes?'

'That almost everyone you will ever meet will set the bar very low. They don't push themselves.'

'Why not?'

'Because they're frightened.'

'Frightened of what?'

'Frightened of failure!'

My expression was taut, my mouth cold.

'I don't want to fail,' I said.

'Nonsense!' Dr. Grimes boomed. 'If you stop fearing failure and start doing things, you'll ultimately succeed!'

'What expedition should I plan?'

Dr. Grimes tugged out a silk handkerchief, blew his nose, grunted, and said:

'One of each I should think.'

'A lost city…?'

'Yes, that's a good start, and a lost treasure, and a plant and animal that are unknown, and a species of butterfly… and what about meteorites as well?'

Fetching a pen and paper from my father's study, I made a list and showed it to Dr. Grimes. Pulling out a monocle, he went through it one item at a time.

'I want you to promise me something,' he said all of a

sudden, his bird-like hand snatching my wrist.

'Something about expeditions?'

'Yes.'

'What?'

'That people will say you can't find a lost city or a treasure... or that you're too young or too unprepared. Every time they doubt you, make up your mind to prove them wrong – do you understand?'

'Yes, Dr. Grimes, I do.'

Slipping away his glasses case, he blew his nose again, and grunted twice.

'The reason to go on an expedition is not to discover about the place you are traversing,' he said. 'But to learn about yourself. Know yourself inside and out and only then will you be the man you're destined to be.'

From: *Expedition: The Anthologies*

# Eye Spy

ONE MORNING, WHILE having breakfast, I opened the copy of my newspaper and focused on the most atrocious and yet enticing image I have ever seen.

A box of prosthetic glass eyes.

Orderly and neat, the eyes were arranged in rows – ten across and five high. Each one was a slightly different size and hue – ranging from chocolate brown to an emerald green.

I assume most people who picked up their copy of the newspaper would have grimaced, winced, and turned the page.

But I couldn't.

I was transfixed.

My wife, Rachana, found me in the kitchen at Dar Khalifa, the newspaper laid over the breakfast table, my face pressed down on the image of the glass eyes.

'Eek!' she squealed.

'I love them,' I whispered. 'And I loathe them, too.'

'They're revolting.'

'I know they are, but I'm drawn to them like nothing I can remember ever being drawn to before.'

'Sounds as though you've just found the subject for your new novel.'

Frowning, I peered up at her, and then down at the eyeballs again.

Rachana was right.

The glass eyes were the perfect first step on a treasure trail.

All day long I stared at the picture of the eyes.

That afternoon, when Timur and Ariane blustered home from school, they found me out on the terrace, the newspaper wide open at the page. Dropping their satchels on the floor, they took in the picture, pointing and giggling.

Ariane asked a hundred questions in five seconds flat.

'Baba's going to write a book about the eyeballs,' Rachana responded firmly.

'*Is he?*' I said.

'Yes he is!'

'What will you call it, Baba?' Ariane asked.

Timur thrust up a hand as though he were in class.

'*Eye Spy,*' he said.

As any creative person will tell you, the essence of creation is a love affair of being bewitched from the inside out.

It's not about the fame and the glory, or about the money you'll make, or won't make. Nor is it about a hundred other things which non-creatives assume to be true. In the way J. D. Salinger had to write because if he did not 'he would turn to stone', creating and creation are a self-therapy, a healing mechanism.

The way I see it, the process of writing is alchemy as much as it is anything else. You take the seed of an idea – in this case a box of glass eyes, you shape it through your imagination, honing it this way and that.

Then, after blending in assorted thoughts, characters, twists and turns, you spew it all out with paper and ink.

*Eye Spy* was a novel written out of a love-hate affair with a simple photograph... a photograph of prosthetic eyes. It would have been easier to have not written it at all. And, were I to have been an author enslaved to a publisher, it would never have been written.

But, the fact I was free, and writing for myself, meant it was not only written, but that it was written how I wanted to write it... and it was done without delay.

As my family and friends will attest, I am drawn to oddity.

I can't help myself.

Few things delight me more than weaving a tapestry from layers of strangeness. And that was exactly what the story I came up with was devised to do.

The greatest eye surgeon of his age, Amadeus Kaine was fêted by celebrities, world leaders, and by despots as well. While treating a particularly odious Central Asian dictator in the presidential palace, he was served a little pie. Curious at its texture and taste, Kaine came to understand it was prepared from eyes gouged from the faces of prisoners in the dictator's opal mines.

Allowing my imagination to zigzag, I spun a tale taking in topics and places I have known. But, most of all, it allowed me to plant a seed and to nurture it.

First, into a seedling.

Then into a sapling.

After that, into a tree with leaves, twigs, branches, and a trunk.

*Eye Spy* was written by me, for me – and *me* alone.

It wasn't geared to getting attention, precious 'Likes' on

social media, or fan mail. Rather, it was about satisfying a deep desire for creation.

A month after first spotting the photograph in the newspaper, I'd thrashed out the story, completed the first draft, and had it edited, too. When ready, it was released with no fanfare at all. Rachana, the kids, and a handful of others knew about it, but no one else.

Birthing it into existence as it was, in a completely low-key way, allowed me to concentrate on what was important – the intense relationship between the author and his work.

When I was a child, the American novelist J. D. Salinger used to visit our home. He was an avid reader of work written by my father, the writer and thinker, Idries Shah. In the decades Salinger used to drop by, he was writing off and on.

But he wasn't publishing.

Having become resigned to writing for himself, I can only imagine he reached the hallowed ground to which every real author aspires...

Perfection.

My belief is that to be truly perfect, a book must be the work of a single person, rather than a group effort that's been hacked around – in the same way that a painter follows their gut, and doesn't continually incorporate the thoughts of others clustered around. In my opinion, a genuine masterpiece of perfection can only be so if it's been experienced solely by the mind that created it.

Far from claiming to be a master worthy of having created a masterpiece, I didn't lock *Eye Spy* away in a safe as Salinger may have done, but published it through my own imprint, Secretum Mundi, the Secret of the World.

From: *Eye Spy*

# Frontier

IN THE DRAWER beside my bed I keep a stack of expired passports.

There are more than a dozen of them, charting zigzagging adventures around all corners of the world. On nights when I can't sleep, I take them out, flick through their pages, and remember the journeys represented in a sea of slapdash immigration stamps.

Last night was one such night.

I'd been tossing and turning for a while, all kinds of thoughts and ideas coursing through my mind. As a way of stirring the flow of memory to wash away my worry, I took out the passports, and selected one.

Issued in 1992, it was cancelled three years later, every available inch of space filled. A picture at the front shows a bright young thing in his mid-twenties in need of much travel to ripen him.

Flicking through the passport, a particular immigration stamp caught my attention. Smudged and inexpertly pressed down on the page, it read 'ENTRY TO TAHIRLAND!' At an angle beside it was a second stamp, which read: 'EXIT FROM TAHIRLAND!'

Before I knew it, I remembered one of the most bizarre expeditions of my life, through the deserts of Upper Egypt and across a frontier like none other.

In a way, the journey had begun in the summer of 1978 at prep school in Tunbridge Wells. An especially wretched master ordered the class to turn to a certain page in the geography textbook. Just before zoning out, I noticed something written at the corner of the page:

'Between Egypt and the Sudan there lies a land known as Bir Tawil, an example of a *Terra Nullius* – a land unclaimed by any nation.'

The rest of the class got down to studying about the emerging nations of post-colonial Africa, while I began fantasizing about venturing to Bir Tawil, and claiming it for myself.

In my experience, the most successful journeys, and the best books, are derived from ideas laid down decades before. There's nothing quite like having something churning away in the back of your head – with you as you work, rest, and sleep.

The *Terra Nullius* of Bir Tawil was one such notion.

I'd often forget about it for years on end. But when something sparked me to remember it, I found a hidden region of my brain had been grinding away at it all along.

Fourteen years after first reading the name of the unwanted land, I became the king of Bir Tawil.

As a traveller there are few delights as gripping as crossing a no-man's land between one country and another. I have always been drawn to the oddity of the way the south of Country A is the north of Country B, and how the east of Country C is the west of Country D.

Likewise, frontiers are man-made fictions that rule our experience of travel. At a time of mass human migration they're in the news more than ever, leading me to frequently revisit the journeys I've made from one nation to the next, across frontiers.

While crossing a no-man's land between Sierra Leone and Liberia, a Polish adventurer once struck up a conversation.

'We are nowhere,' he said.

'Nowhere and everywhere,' I added.

The Pole sighed lugubriously.

'What joy it is to reach a frontier filled with hope of what will come next,' he said.

From: *Frontier: The Anthologies*

# Godman

GODMAN IS A book born inside me.

I like to think the story grew as I grew, travelled as I travelled, and learned as I learned. As anyone who's read my *Sorcerer's Apprentice* knows, an Indian magician visited our home in the English countryside when I was a child. The guardian of my ancestor's tomb, he was a great hulking Pashtun named Hafiz Jan. While all my friends were out on their skateboards, I was learning magic under his doting gaze.

Hafiz Jan was eventually banished.

One of his magic tricks went terribly wrong, leading to my parents and sisters almost being incinerated by a fireball. The illusions I learned, which were the type developed by Harry Houdini, and used by India's so-called 'godmen', were based on shockingly dangerous chemical reactions. But for a child in a dull English village, they were a thing of ultimate wonder.

When my beloved Hafiz Jan left, retracing his way back to northern India by land, along with his tea-crate filled with chemicals, I vowed that one day when I was old enough, I would seek him out and learn the magic of the godmen.

I am pleased to say that's exactly what I did.

During the months I spent in India learning about magical illusion – a time which eventually formed the basis of *Sorcerer's Apprentice* – I grasped how virtually anyone with a box of chemicals, and the right spiel, could set themselves up with a livelihood. Success didn't depend so much on skill, but on the audience's faith.

Or, rather, their need to believe.

Over the years I have witnessed the most extraordinary feats of illusion performed in great halls with devotees numbering in their thousands, and on railway tracks where I was the only person watching. I've been spellbound by performances, and have winced as well, especially when tricks floundered as they frequently tend to do.

Although I only wrote *Godman* in the last few months, the story came to me on a freezing morning outside Lucknow in the mid-nineties. I'd spent the night in a traveller's hovel, waiting for a holy man named 'Trapat Guru' to appear. Everyone I had asked waxed lyrical about him, declaring him to be a 'saviour', as though all the other godmen were fraudsters.

After much waiting, Trapat Guru finally turned up.

The very last person I expected him to be, he was in his thirties, long-limbed and gangly, with a ready smile. But it wasn't his age or physical characteristics that struck me.

Rather, it was his voice.

Until that morning, all the established godmen, or aspiring godmen, I'd encountered were Indian born and bred. Trapat Guru was quite different. He looked Indian, but had a thick Glaswegian accent.

News of the holy man's arrival spread fast and, as tends to happen in rural India, a crowd gathered fast. People streamed from their homes, milling about, waiting for the action.

Joining them, I watched.

First, Trapat Guru blessed the throng. Then he performed a series of tricks – advertised as 'miracles'. After that, he treated a dozen or so of the villagers, for everything from aches and pains, to deafness. At the end of the routine, Trapat Guru handed out homemade amulets, and received small donations in return.

As though we were two members of a similar fraternity, I couldn't help but be drawn to him. While I'd been learning about magic and illusion in Kolkata out of sheer interest, he was apparently using the same skills to support himself.

I didn't go over and strike up a conversation, because it risked unmasking him. Although I disapproved of what he was doing, he was relieving boredom, and didn't seem to be harming anyone.

Instead, I found myself fantasizing about a story in which a down-on-his-luck magician from England went to the subcontinent, and became a godman superstar. That's how my novel, *Godman*, came about.

Ten years ago I was visiting Scotland for a literary festival, and stayed in Edinburgh for a few days. The city has always inspired me enormously, and is where my grandparents met during the Great War.

While in town I looked up an old writer friend, and followed him to his favourite pub. A dingy backstreet haunt, it was the kind of place I'd usually be keen to avoid.

But my friend insisted we go there, so we did.

We hadn't been inside for more than a few minutes when the landlord announced that a magician would be performing.

Without further ado, Trapat Guru stepped out.

Recognizing him at once, I was propelled back to the patch of open ground west of Lucknow. He looked older, of course, but it was unmistakably him.

Same ready smile, same long limbs, same thick Glaswegian accent.

This time, I couldn't give up the chance to make contact. So, when the routine was over, I introduced myself.

'I'm Arnie,' he smiled. 'I read your book, *Sorcerer's Apprentice.*'

'I saw you performing near Lucknow,' I said. 'Was you, wasn't it?'

Arnie blushed, winced, and nodded.

'I never took the donations,' he said, as though he was expecting me to condemn him.

'I'm sure you didn't.'

Leaning forward, the magician pulled a playing card from my ear.

The ten of hearts.

'I'm not a magician at all,' he confided.

'Well, I was impressed by your routine,' I answered brightly.

'That's not quite what I mean.'

'Then what are you if you're not a magician?'

'I'm an anthropologist,' Arnie said.

He explained how he'd spent six months crisscrossing India, doing tricks as a way to study people.

I asked what his conclusions had been.

Arnie looked at me hard, his eyes honest and wide.

'I learned that just as they need food and water,' he said, 'people need to believe.'

'So you were merely providing a service?'

'Exactly,' said Arnie. 'I was a dream maker.'

From: *Godman*

# Hinterland

WHEN I WAS a child, I read a story about a fearless explorer named Jonjo who had crisscrossed every corner of the globe in search of treasure.

Jonjo was fearful of nothing, and there were no lengths to which he would not go to track down the treasure at hand.

One day, someone asked Jonjo to reveal his secret, for he'd managed to find treasure on a scale unmatched by anyone else – dead or alive.

Jonjo thought long and hard, then he said:

'The secret of finding treasure is looking inland.'

Taking the book from home to school and from school to home, I told everyone I met about Jonjo's secret:

'You have to look inland,' I would tell them, 'otherwise you won't find treasure.'

On receiving the information, some people reacted in gratitude. But most of them laughed at me. They said I was an idiot for spouting nonsense, and that my young age was no excuse at all.

Luckily for me, I never listened to those who pushed me down or mocked Jonjo and his wisdom.

Instead, I found myself turning the fragment of truth over in my head. While other children dreamt of Lego, I dreamt of a world inland – a realm set far from the shore.

One day at Langton House, where I grew up, a visiting elderly gentleman asked me about my interests. I told him that the only thing I was really interested in was searching for treasure inland rather than at the coast.

'You mean in the hinterland?' he asked.

'*Hinterland?*'

'The hinterland… A place that's far inland.'

I've heard of famous scientists or painters being touched by a seminal moment in their childhood. That was it for me. My ears sucked the word in – *Hinterland* – my mind's voice playing it over and over like a mantra.

Weeks passed, and the book with Jonjo's story was put on a shelf too high for me to reach, probably in the hope that I would move on to a fresh obsession. But I knew the tale so well I no longer actually needed it in my hand and, in any case, the way I told it to myself had improved on the real thing.

I would tell anyone and everyone who'd listen that I was going to the HINTERLAND! The way I said it, and thought about it, the word was written in capitals with an exclamation at the end.

HINTERLAND! – the realm of Jonjo's treasure…

I regarded the hinterland as a country blessed with all kinds of riches.

Go inland and you encounter subtle differences from the world beyond the shore. Point yourself in the direction of the interior and you find yourself on a trajectory that can only end in wonder – whether it be a cultural treasure, or one fashioned from gold, fit for Jonjo himself.

From: *Hinterland: The Anthologies*

## House of the Tiger King

WHEN IT COMES to lost-city jungle expeditions, there's nothing quite so irresistible as hindsight.

The journey that eventually became the book *House of the Tiger King*, and the feature documentary of the same name, stretched to sixteen weeks in deep jungle, or rather cloud forest.

To the uninitiated, it's almost impossible to explain the challenges of that quixotic realm. From the moment you arrive, everything is trying to end your life and, more importantly, to devour you.

The jungle is a lost-city-explorer eating machine.

Clambering forward with a mountain of equipment, with dozens of porters, and with a full film crew, not to mention the ordeal of searching for a lost city, you cannot help but find yourself succumbing to delirium.

Looking back at it after a considerable interlude, I grasp how *House of the Tiger King* was not about the jungle itself, but about the relationships, the trials and tribulations, of what was an insufferably arduous expedition.

But, for most of it, it was about the mania.

While writing the book, I referred time and again to Joseph Conrad's classic *Heart of Darkness*. Reading a few pages of that glorious pithy novel each morning before I started to write eased me into the mindset like nothing else.

Having experienced my own parallel version of Marlow's fateful journey upriver in search of Kurtz, I found that I sucked the pages in, breathing them, as though I understood the tale in a way no one else alive could ever do.

A veteran of the African Congo, Joseph Conrad was a novelist who walked an ultra-taut tightrope of extraordinary and mesmerizing skill. I've often imagined him sitting at his desk, steel-nib dip pen in hand, scratching out the lines that became the sensation they did.

A great many novelists write from experience, but Conrad's devotion to the process surpassed almost all the rest. He managed to slip back into the version of himself that mile by mile had struggled up the great snaking wrath of the Congo River.

I planned to work for four weeks on *House of the Tiger King* in a little attic room at an old school-friend's house. The building was on the market, and was empty, except when prospective buyers turned up to view it.

Before starting the first chapter, I reflected on my hero, Joseph Conrad, and how I could recreate the mania that characterized my expedition, just as he'd done.

I pulled out a picture of myself at the height of the journey, on a tributary of Madre de Dios. My face was pocked with sores, my clothing was shredded and wet, and my expression was one of absolute anguish, as though the world around me was about to implode. Having studied the photo, I glanced at myself in the full-length mirror behind the door.

I was clean, happy, and well fed.

'This won't do,' I cried out loud. 'It won't do at all!'

Turning the problem over in my mind, I came up with an idea:

I'd regress to the state I was in while searching for the lost city of Paititi, the so-called 'House of the Tiger King'.

The first thing I did was to dig out the boots and clothes I'd worn in the jungle. Having soaked them in cold water, I went down to the garden and buried them in mud all afternoon.

Then I called a pal who worked at London's Hospital for Tropical Diseases.

After a lot of begging on my part, he held out a jar packed with anopheles mosquitoes, with the words 'I could be fired by the department head for this!'

Next, I filled the attic with pots of water, sealed the windows, and turned up the heating full blast.

Once the temperature was at thirty-eight degrees, and condensation was dripping down the windows, I tapped the open jar of mosquitoes onto the floor.

An hour later, having downloaded a looped audio track of the cloud forest, I sat down at my desk, and began to write.

As the first week ground on, I cursed myself for being such a nutcase, and for not merely imagining the conditions as any other author might have done.

Thrilled beyond all reason at being freed from a laboratory cage, the mosquitoes began eating me alive. In keeping with the original jungle journey, I scratched the bites as much as I could, and rubbed dirt into them, so they would get infected.

By the second week, I was slipping into bouts of delirium.

Going around the corner to my own comfortable bed had seemed like cheating. So, at the start of the second week, I brought a sleeping bag over to the attic, and slept in there, too. I considered shunning the loo, and digging holes in the garden, but my friend, whose house I was using, was prudish by nature, so I refrained.

He was so prudish, that we all called him 'Prudy'.

As it was, things got rather awkward when, at the end of the second week, a well-dressed couple who were interested in the house dropped by to view it.

They found me stripped down to my boxer shorts, peppered in infected mosquito bites, my eyes circled with dark rings.

The woman, who was heavily pregnant, asked to see the attic.

'Might not be a good idea,' I said.

'May I enquire why?'

'Because I've recreated a particular bend on the Madre de Dios River up there.'

'Whatever for?' they both asked at once.

Looking at them hard, I swallowed anxiously, and said:

'So as to be authentic to my craft.'

By the third week, I'd broken the back of the manuscript.

On the Tuesday morning, the school friend who'd loaned me the attic came by unannounced. I got the feeling he'd had a garbled report from the prospective buyers, who'd apparently been scared off.

Annoyingly, he turned up just as I'd pushed the boundaries of my regime...

Having become quite used to being eaten alive by mosquitoes, I'd managed to trap about fifty wasps, and had introduced them into the attic room, along with ten poison arrow frogs, which I'd rented from an exotic pet shop on the South Bank.

With the new additions to my attic jungle in place, I got back to work.

But, as I hammered out my daily wordage, something struck me.

I'd totally overlooked stomach trouble.

The single most ubiquitous element characterizing the sixteen weeks of utter jungle misery was being hounded by food poisoning, and riddled with guinea worms.

Without delay, I hurried to a particularly vile provisions emporium on the bad end of Brick Lane, and rooted through the chilling cabinet at the front. I'd often heard customers bemoaning how they'd got the runs from the frozen packs of mixed fish offcuts, weeks past their sell-by date.

Handing over a crisp £5 note, I bought two kilos, and took them back to the attic. Once they'd thawed out, they stunk the place up so greatly that my eyes watered.

Even the mosquitoes, frogs, and wasps seemed displeased.

Cooking up the fish on a camping stove for a couple of minutes, I blew on the meat to cool it, and gobbled it down, while doing my level best to avoid the inevitable gag reflex.

Within an hour, the rotten offcuts had coursed their way through my alimentary canal and had been ejected, leaving me clutching my stomach.

It was at this moment that Prudy arrived.

Putting his head around the door, he winced. As he did so, a wasp stung him slap bang in the middle of his forehead.

'What the frigging heck's going on, old boy?!'

'I've recreated the jungle,' I said brightly. 'You know, for authenticity. I've even got the runs!'

'This won't do!'

My face fell.

'D'you think I should have got dengue fever again... you know, for total effect?'

Prudy regarded me with rage.

'I want the jungle out of here by five p.m.,' he said.

'But I've paid for the frogs for another week,' I whimpered. 'And God knows how I'll get the mosquitoes back in the jar. There are so many of them. Think they've been breeding.'

Dabbing a handkerchief to the wasp sting, Prudy didn't seem to be listening. In silence, he jerked a thumb to the copy of Joseph Conrad's classic, sitting in pride of place on the desk.

'I'm sure *he* never needed to recreate it all like you're doing.'

'Of course he didn't,' I shot back. 'But *he* was the real thing!'

From: *House of the Tiger King*

# In Arabian Nights

A COUPLE OF weeks ago, a wizened old man turned up at Dar Khalifa and asked to see me.

By good fortune, I happened to be passing the front door at that moment, and overheard the guardians explaining that I was tied down writing a book – which indeed I was.

The man said:

'Please tell Monsieur Tahir that I have something for him.'

'*What?*'

'A map.'

I may well have gone back to my desk, but there's almost nothing that excites me so greatly as maps. I've been obsessed with them since I was a very young child.

So I went out, greeted the man, and invited him inside.

Her inbuilt radar having sensed a potential intruder, our housekeeper Zohra burst out from the kitchen, and circled around the sofa on which I was sitting with the guest.

In his own time, the man, who said his name was Seif, stuck a hand down the front of his trousers and pulled out a packet.

Furled up in brown paper and string, it looked ancient.

As I watched, the packaging was pulled away.

Inside, bound in dark green boards, was a folded map. Before I could ask questions or make a comment of any kind, Seif opened the sheet out.

The first thing I noticed was that, in line with the very best maps, it was backed on canvas. The second thing that piqued my curiosity was what looked like a spatter of dried blood on the top right corner.

The visitor scratched the nail of a forefinger down his cheek, his chapped lips parting.

'It has been protected,' he said.

'What's it a map of?' I asked, craning my neck to try and make sense of the place names and the lines.

'A landscape.'

'Yes, but where is it... *Morocco*?'

'No.'

'Then where?'

'It's not a map of a place.'

'I don't understand... there are names... and I can see rivers and mountains.'

A hint of a smile slipped over the chapped lips.

'A map doesn't need to be rooted in a place that exists,' the visitor said.

'You mean it's an imaginary map.'

'Yes, and then again, no.'

'It has to be one or the other – fact or fantasy,' I said.

'I do not believe that it does,' he answered.

Holding the map into the light, I took in the details. With keen interest, I observed the way it had clearly defined regions, each one set apart from the others, as though forced to be separate. And, I noticed how there was what I can only describe as a sense of dark brooding in certain areas – as though evil awaited there.

Despite our brief discussion, I was still confused as to what the map was all about.

Before I could ask yet again, Seif said:

'This is a map of stories.'

'Stories? What kind of stories?'

'The stories I was told by my father as a child… the same stories he was told by his father, and his father was told before him.'

'How wonderful.'

The visitor shook his head from side to side.

'No, it's not,' he declared.

'Why not?'

'Because a story map such as this must be passed on through the generations, so it can continue on its own journey.'

'It sounds as though that's what's happened.'

'Yes, but the road is about to end.'

Again, I was confused.

'Have you thought of passing the map on to your own children?'

'That's the problem… I have never been married.'

'Can't you give it to a nephew or niece?'

Again, the visitor shook his head.

'They're not interested. At least they're not interested in the fact that the map is a map of stories. If I left it to them, they would simply sell it.'

I winced.

'That would be a great pity,' I said.

'I came to Dar Khalifa,' Seif explained. 'Because someone told me you are the King of the Storytellers.'

'I'm certainly not that. I'm not even a Prince of

Storytellers.' I smiled. 'Perhaps, if you were being generous, you could say that I'm a lowly squire...'

'The Squire of the Storytellers?'

'Yes. That's what I am.'

'But you love stories as much as you love maps?'

I nodded eagerly.

'Adore them both.'

'Then,' Seif said, 'I would be grateful if you could take the map as a gift, and look after it.'

'But it's the map of *your* family.'

The visitor turned the sheet over and pointed to a line of Arabic script on the back.

'Look there.'

Squinting, I tried to make sense of the words.

'Looks like a name.'

'Yes, that's what it is... a name.'

'Whose name?'

'The name of the family that began the story map.'

'You think they passed it on to your ancestors?'

'Yes.'

'But why?'

'Because they had no one left to tell stories.'

Without another word, Seif pulled out a pen, and wrote a line of text on the back on the sheet.

'Take care of it well,' he said, after a long silence. 'Add to it and, most importantly, make sure it is passed on to your children and grandchildren.'

I wrote *In Arabian Nights* because I knew no keener way to

understand Morocco than through the lens of stories and storytelling.

Even though I was born and brought up in the West, I was weaned on an Oriental mindset – constantly reminded that the culture in which we were living was in its infancy.

I have dozens of books written by Europeans on the subject of Morocco and Moroccan society. Almost all of them consider the culture straight on, as though staring at it eye to eye.

While all those books certainly have layers of interest, they're terribly limited. The reason is because the authors were trapped. They'd trapped themselves – into a rigidity of understanding, the kind that has paralyzed the West.

Through the pages of *In Arabian Nights*, I allowed myself to slip into the labyrinth of stories.

This labyrinth is everywhere – whether it be in the tales Zohra told my children while they ate their meals, in the medinas of Marrakech and Fès, or on the story maps, such as the one Seif presented to me the other day.

Visible to those who believe in it, the labyrinth enables and powers a society that's solid right down to the core.

They're two inseparable halves of the very same thing.

Its tales *are* Morocco, just as Morocco *is* the tales.

From: *In Arabian Nights*

## In Search of King Solomon's Mines

MY FAVOURITE ARAB proverb goes, 'Much travel is needed before the raw man is ripened.'

If ever there were a raw man who needed ripening, it was me when I first arrived in the Ethiopian capital, Addis Ababa. I was in my mid-thirties and, while I'd embarked on all manner of intrepid adventures, I was in desperate need of seasoning.

I'm a diehard believer that journeys are life-lessons, and that those of us who have not been pitted against ourselves through travel are far poorer for it. Roam through foreign lands with fresh eyes and you're stretched in ways that no other experience can ever match.

My friend Sir Wilfred Thesiger first suggested I visit Ethiopia, the land of his birth. He said I'd find a culture that had changed little in millennia, and was true to itself. Thinking about it now, I'm certain he had sized me up as being untested by life. While I had hoped Ethiopia was a destination that might provide answers to the riddle of King Solomon's mines, I perceive now that he saw it as a realm in which I could come of age.

Without doubt Africa's most mysterious country, Ethiopia is a magical crucible of folklore and culture. From the moment of my arrival, I was transfixed. It was as though I'd stepped into a parallel universe in which nothing was quite what it seemed.

What better tool to take me there than my family's obsession with the search for King Solomon's mines? The mission afforded me the opportunity of drilling down into the country's cultural bedrock – in a way that a tourist could never hope to do.

Anyone who was alive in the eighties will remember the nightly news bulletins – the ones that shocked the world and led to Live Aid.

The Ethiopia I encountered was one created by decades of famine, war, endemic corruption, and a grim struggle for life that touched one and all. But not until I planted my own two feet upon its soil could I begin to understand what the television news segments failed to show.

Ethiopia had been shrouded from the rest of the African continent for decades. Visiting it was like passing through a looking glass into a gentle land sleeping under a witch's spell.

My zigzagging journeys through Ethiopia in search of King Solomon's mines took place almost twenty years ago. I'm thrilled to report that, since then, the country has opened up, prospered, and begun the long march towards its future.

At the time of writing, the nation's infrastructure is being rebuilt. Plush new roads fan out from Addis Ababa, and there are even high-speed trains to Djibouti – both unthinkable in the days of my own journeys.

Of course, in Africa, a nation's good intentions can be halted in a heartbeat. There's nothing to say that progress won't be stopped in its tracks.

But, as I reflect on Ethiopia, a land which I hold so dear, I like to live in hope.

When this book was released, three things happened that surprised me.

The first was that Channel 4's 'To the Ends of the Earth' series, and National Geographic Television, asked me to return to Ethiopia... to do the journeys over again.

I remember receiving the call, and wondering what Thesiger would have said to the proposal. He'd have told the producers to go stick their budget and leave him in peace. But, being far more egotistical than Sir Wilfred, I discussed the idea, and worked with a production company, which put together a team.

*The Search for King Solomon's Mines* was the first documentary I presented. Until then I'd done almost no television work.

TV couldn't be more at odds with the lot of the writer.

With a film team in tow, you stick out like a sore thumb. Far worse, though, is that you're suddenly shoved out of the loop in terms of the decision-making process.

Although well-meaning, the director, who doubled as a cameraman, and the young Irish producer, had never worked anywhere with the faintest hint of adversity. We spent five weeks crisscrossing Ethiopia, with Samson, Bahru, and me doing our best to seem enthused.

The truth, of course, was that we'd been turned from second-rate adventurers into third-rate actors pretending to be second-rate adventurers.

One night, while driving through bandit territory in southern Ethiopia, the Emperor's Jeep slalomed into what looked like a puddle.

Within seconds, liquid mud was up to the doors.

Bahru accelerated hard, but the Jeep merely got embedded all the more deeply.

Pulling out a satellite phone, the director called London, and got through to the production company's project coordination. A pleasant young man with a ready smile, he was out on a date when the call came in… A call ordering him to get the Ethiopian authorities to scramble emergency services.

Naturally, it being Ethiopia, and the road being infested with bandits, he couldn't scramble anyone. Although, as I understand it, his date melted with delight at the evening's high drama.

The Irish producer, whose last job had been on *The Big Breakfast*, was naturally terrified of being attacked and raped. I have a vivid memory of her tucking her hair up into a cap and rubbing charcoal on her face to look like a man. As she struggled to disguise herself, Bahru stripped down to his underpants, and dived in under the Jeep.

A driver in tune with his vehicle, he understood that nothing would move the Jeep on until the liquid mud had been drained.

Eventually, the mud was cleared, and we made it to the next village without becoming another statistic on the bandit-attack chart.

The second thing that happened after *In Search of King Solomon's Mines* was launched was that I received a letter with a Somerset postmark and a return address sticker with

'Mr. & Mrs. Hayter' written in block capitals at the top.

Opening it, I discovered it was from the son of the pre-War adventurer, the inimitable Frank Hayter. Hoping to have some of the many gaps filled in, I invited him to lunch at my club in London.

A frail man with a hesitant air, he told me that his father had died in the nineties, and that, having left Africa, he'd become a poultry farmer.

'Did he raise you with tales of his exploits in the wilds of Ethiopia?' I asked.

Frank Hayter's son looked at me hard, his eyes watering.

'No,' he said softly. 'Never mentioned his journeys.'

'*Never?*'

'No.'

'I wonder why.'

'Because he'd got Africa out of his system,' he said.

The third surprising thing that happened took place three years after the book's launch.

Ask any writer with more than a few books under their belt, and they'll almost certainly tell you they get lots of correspondence from readers. Unlike many authors, I love hearing from my readers, even when they're crazy – which in my case they often seem to be.

One morning I woke up early, and went through the usual assortment of incoming emails. One of the first messages I came to scrolled on for pages and pages.

It began:

'Dear Tahir Shah, please read this. I promise you I'm not

nuts. If you don't believe me, check the email address I'm using...'

Scrolling to the top of the page, I checked the email address.

It was from someone at the Boeing Corporation.

Raising an eyebrow, I read the message.

It turned out that a senior executive at Boeing Commercial Aviation had taken a liking to my book on Ethiopia.

Hell, he'd taken more than a liking to it – he ADORED it. It wouldn't be an exaggeration to say he was obsessed with *In Search of King Solomon's Mines*.

His email, which went on and on over pages, explained how he was charged with selling what was then Boeing's latest sensation, the Dreamliner 787, to fleets around the world.

Having read my book, he felt drawn to Ethiopia. And, having been drawn to Ethiopia, he developed a tie-up to supply the cutting-edge fleet of Dreamliners to Ethiopian Airlines.

Hearing the news, I smiled to myself. It'd been Ethiopian Airlines' inflight magazine, *Selamta*, that my old nemesis Mohamed Amin had run. For years I'd been paid by him in tickets on Ethiopian Airlines.

Flattered at being a small cog in a big system – a system that served many of the world's airlines, I replied at once.

An hour later, a second email from the sales executive appeared in my inbox. Whereas the previous message had been sent from Seattle, the second one had been typed out a mile and a half away, in downtown Casablanca.

This time I raised both eyebrows.

Reading the message, I learned that the executive, whose name was Ihssane Mounir, was a Moroccan who'd emigrated to the United States years before, and had clawed his way up the totem pole of Boeing's Commercial Aviation structure.

I invited Ihssane to Dar Khalifa that afternoon. Clean cut, and with mountains of irresistible charm, he turned up, hugged me like an old friend, and explained how he hadn't known I was living in Casablanca – the city he was travelling to when he sent his message.

That afternoon, Ihssane told me about his life, which was like something from *A Thousand and One Nights*. Born into a respected family from Rabat, his father had been a calligrapher at the Royal Court. A similar age to the Crown Prince Mohammed, Ihssane was invited to attend the little school in the palace, at which the future King and his brother took daily lessons.

As a result, Ihssane became well acquainted with the current King, and his brother, Moulay Rachid. Everything went well, until that is Ihssane developed asthma, which was aggravated by the capital's humid Atlantic air.

A physician was called for. He examined the boy and made his diagnosis. His treatment would be to go into the Moroccan hinterland to live with his relatives in Errachidia, where the air was drier than dry.

Ihssane was immediately dispatched, and spent months and then years in Errachidia, returning to the Royal Court to visit the Crown Prince and his brother whenever he could.

Had he been brought up solely in the palace, the young

Ihssane Mounir may have developed delusions of grandeur. But, having been torn away and dealt a far simpler life in the kingdom's desert interior, he learned something that I value very greatly indeed.

I call it 'Full Spectrum Living'.

Ihssane had picked up the etiquette of the Royal Court, the ways of the desert, and everything in between. As a result, he was softly spoken and worldly in a way that I've rarely encountered.

Over the afternoon he visited Dar Khalifa, we chatted about all kinds of things, from the scent of the rain in the Sahara, to curious American customs which delighted but confused us both.

As afternoon ebbed toward evening he looked at me hard, and asked:

'Would you come to Ethiopia with us, as a guest of Boeing?'

'Who's us?'

'Me, a few folks from Boeing, and our CEO, Alan Mulally.'

I agreed, and a few days later arrived at Addis Ababa's Bole Airport, where Samson was waiting for me.

'Don't ask me to search for the gold mines, again,' he said.

'Don't worry, I won't,' I replied. 'That journey's done and dusted.'

Samson led the way to his battered old Lada taxi.

'Hotel Ghion?'

I winced.

'Not this time my old friend,' I said. 'Boeing's paying…

which means it's the Sheraton.'

That evening, I had dinner with Boeing's CEO. He'd flown in that afternoon with his SWAT team.

'Read your book twice,' he said. 'It was a triumph.'

'Then you can understand that I'm not accustomed to luxury like this,' I said.

Mulally glanced over at me, his lips warm with a smile.

'Luxury's meaningless,' he said. 'What matters are those you count as friends.'

Next day we were invited to the Presidential Palace, where all the stops had been pulled out. A kitsch 1960s extravaganza built for Haile Selassie, the former Emperor, it was desperately threadbare.

The President, Girma Wolde-Giorgis, was waiting for us in one of the great halls.

Having been introduced, I strode forwards.

The President flinched.

No surprise, as he'd banned my book on Ethiopia for including a short condemnatory paragraph about his government.

'Go on, Mr. President,' Mulally said brightly, 'won't ya give Tahir Shah a nice Ethiopian hug?!'

Scowling, the President pulled me close, and the cameras clicked.

Once the photo-op was over, we were taken around the palace.

The tour included a visit to Haile Selassie's private apartment. We got ushered into his bedroom, in which everything had been left just as it was when the wretched dictator Mengistu Haile Mariam had him taken out and killed.

Curious, I opened one of the cupboards, and found a line of neatly pressed white uniforms, the chest of each adorned with rows of medal ribbons.

Next on the tour were the Imperial garages, in which dozens of bullet-proofed Cadillacs were ready for use. After that, the *pièce de résistance*, the treasure vaults of Imperial Ethiopia.

I've seen a lot of things in my time, and am shamelessly unimpressed with bling-bling. In any case, jewels aren't my thing. But what I found in the treasure vaults under the palace wooed me and wowed me like nothing I've ever encountered.

Arranged on racks were the crowns of the Ethiopian Emperors, as well as relics from the nation's most distant past. There were gem-encrusted orbs, icons, ceremonial standards, enormous silver crosses, ancient Ge'ez Bibles, and innumerable gifts from emperors, presidents and kings.

At the back of the treasure vault I found a large signed photograph of Jackie Onassis, along with a little phial of moon dust, presented to Haile Selassie by NASA.

Trawling through loot, my former quest – to locate the gold mines of King Solomon – fell sharply into focus.

Sometimes in life you can only understand a puzzle when the right pieces are put on display. That's certainly been my recurring experience, and it was never truer than in my life-long fascination with the source of Solomon's wealth.

The extraordinary and ancient wealth of Ethiopia was not

made from gold, or even gems, but rather from the cultural fabric of the society I'd come to know, respect, and love.

From: *In Search of King Solomon's Mines*

# India

THIRTY YEARS AGO almost to the day, I arrived in India for the first time.

Looking back to that morning, I could never have imagined that India would become such a cornerstone of my life. I was twenty-two years old, enthusiastic for adventure and desperate to experience the interwoven layers of life that only raw and unrestrained travel can provide. Seeing with fresh eyes is the great gift of a traveller, and seeing India for the first time is surely the most all-encompassing gift of all.

Having taken the cheapest flight I could find, on Iraqi Airways via Baghdad, I arrived in Mumbai at dawn. The first thing that hit me was the smell. Not the smell of sewage or even perfume, but the smell of a kind of ammonia-based cleaning product – not unlike mothballs. The airport seemed to have been hosed down in that smell. Mumbai – then Bombay – now has a flash new airport terminal building, but the smell is still exactly the same.

On an almost non-existent budget, I took the local bus into the city that first morning, and began on a treasure trail that has characterized every journey I've made to India since. Having married into a Mumbai-based family, I have found myself washed there by the prevailing winds with great regularity. At times I have even based myself in India, living there for many months at a stretch.

If experienced correctly, India is like a tonic – so powerful and so intoxicating that one needs to withdraw from time to time to regroup and decompress, before entering the slipstream once again.

By nature, I tend to notice details – every single detail. I can't help it. That means I lap up each fragment of information passed to my mind through my senses. I see every scratch on every battered old bus, every fly, and spot of dirt, every rose petal thrown at a deity's feet, and each and every pilgrim caught up at the Kumbh Mela or other such throng.

As a result, I get utterly exhausted by the sensory overload. After three or four days I can usually be found slumped in a cane chair out on the lawn at Mumbai's Willingdon Club, my eyes wide, my mind straining to process the individual strands of what I've seen.

A curse has affected me at various times of my life – the curse of not noticing the full bandwidth of India's majesty. Like someone who's been kept awake for days and nights, exposed to a thousand episodes of their favourite TV serial, I have to sit in a darkened room or else I'll miss out by regarding it as normal.

Over a period of the thirty years I have had the honour to know the subcontinent, I've taken great pleasure in searching out corners of life and experience not usually accessed by others. I'm far more interested in hearing the life story of a man making *jalaibees* on a Kolkata street corner than knowing the kind of stuff well-heeled travel writers tend to note down.

For me, India is the ultimate cultural and sensory Mothership.

Those of us who've been lucky enough to have viewed

its secret corners sometimes like to imagine we know a great deal more than we actually do. For me that's the ultimate delight – the fact that however many lifetimes I will ever live, or however many millions of miles my feet will ever walk, I will never be able to do anything more than scratch the surface.

For that, I owe India everything.

From: *India: The Anthologies*

# India Considered

I LIKE TO think of a travelling life as a mosaic pattern, the kind that adorns the fountains in the rambling Moroccan labyrinth that has been my home through the last dozen years and more.

Observed from a distance, it is a study in gentle and serene elegance.

Different colours, interwoven shapes and varying motifs, conjuring an expression of beauty that tantalizes one's sight, as the sound of trickling water soothes the soul.

But draw in closer, and the effect changes.

As one nears, inch by inch, a secret world is revealed.

A world formed from detail.

The tiniest fragments of mosaic, shaped with absolute skill, form patterns and sub-patterns, like the strokes made by an artist's brush.

I am enchanted by the mastery of the mosaic makers. I love to observe how each individual fragment has been cleaved into the perfect outline, so that it lies snug with the others around it.

In the way that I perceive the world, the mosaics themselves are the journeys I have made. They are the countries my feet have traversed. The experiences that have in their own way fashioned me deep-down, from the inside out.

But, stare at the mosaic fountain long enough, and you begin to distinguish another layer... a dimension that was previously concealed.

Most artists cling to what is obvious, drawing delight in the onion's outer-most layers. While doing so, they fail to understand that there is not one, two, or even three layers, but many hundreds – lying beneath the surface, waiting to be discovered.

Although enchanted by the mosaics themselves, I have come to appreciate that they are neither the thing of greatest beauty, nor of real significance. They are the delicious flesh of the peach, but not the stone.

Look beyond the mosaics, focus on the slender lines that hold them in place, and you observe the thing of true value.

And so it is with travel.

To almost anyone who set eyes on a mosaic fountain, the grouting is invisible.

As with travel, we mesmerize those around us with tales of grand experience, adventure, and even bravery. We recount exploits tinged with intrigue, our stories framed in superlatives.

Yet, as we do so, we fail to pass on the kind of details which make the path of a lone traveller into an experience that shapes one from the inside out.

For me, it's the onion's deepest layers that hold the greatest riches.

Layers that are rarely the easiest to uncover or understand.

But, tease them out, decipher them, and a world comes into sharp focus that is more fantastical than anything untrammelled vision could ever discern.

Through my own journeys, detail has been both my currency and my matrix of discovery: the way I have sought to take inspiration from the lands that have passed beneath my feet.

As I sit here, pondering the subject, a memory is nudging me:

A long while ago I was studying magic in Kolkata. It was the kind of thing that so-called 'godmen' pass off as *real* magic, a realm pioneered by Harry Houdini a century ago. My magician master, a sadist called Hakim Feroze, insisted that I search for detail. Without it, he said, I could never hope to understand the rich textures of his illusionary world.

One afternoon, I came to be sitting at a Kolkata café. It wasn't much more than a cluster of tables and benches in the sidewalk's shade. I'd been sitting there for hours, having decided not to leave until I glimpsed something that wasn't obvious.

Anyone who's been to India will know that there's never any shortage of fodder to amaze and entertain. But what I was looking for wasn't the wild rumpus of life so overwhelming to the newly arrived.

I was searching for a whole other level.

So for the thousandth time I glanced out at the street, and found myself looking at an old woman and a cow. It's something you see across the subcontinent and isn't very unusual at all.

People paid a rupee or so to the woman, who sold them a handful of succulent green grass, which they fed to the cow.

I stared and I stared, and I stared and I stared.

And, as I stared, I took notice of the details:

The bright orange colour of the woman's *sari*.

The mottled pattern of the cow's hide.

And the way the grass had been heaped up.

The more I looked at it, the more I began to think it was ordinary. I'd been looking at it for so long that I wasn't doing more than scratching the surface.

But suddenly, it was as though something shifted inside me – as if a gear lever had been moved.

At that moment, I worked out what was really going on:

The woman didn't own the cow – the milkman did. But, after milking the animal in the early morning, he wanted to go around selling the milk. So, he rented the cow to the old woman. Each morning she'd pluck some grass in a field, and would lead the creature to the city.

As I had seen, people would pay her a rupee or two for some grass, and feed it to the cow.

By deciphering the system, I witnessed a genius – a genius that served everyone:

The milkman was happy because he was paid for having his cow looked after and fed all day.

The woman was happy because she had a livelihood.

The passers-by were happy because they received divine blessings for feeding a sacred animal.

But, best of all, the cow was thrilled because she was getting fed and loved by everyone all day long.

As with the memory of that street scene in Kolkata, or the pattern of the mosaic fountain, I like to delve down deep.

To search for the story behind the story, and question what the senses feed us.

After all, the most intoxicating value of life is surely to discover that which has been earned – by challenging what we hold to be true.

From: *Document Journal*

# Journey Through Namibia

NAMIBIA IS ONE of Africa's youngest and most mysterious nations, a land of daunting size and rugged beauty. Within its realm contrasts abound. Rocky plateaux rise hard by expansive deserts; lush watercourses give way to barren vistas and ancient peoples brush with modern technology.

In Namibia's vast desert regions some of the world's most enduring plants, creatures and peoples abide according to an archaic natural scheme. Into these endless tracts, nature cast her richest treasures – diamonds, other precious stones and minerals. Today the country accounts for roughly one-sixth of the world's diamond wealth.

Records from the time of Herodotus indicate that the Phoenicians were the first explorers to circumnavigate the African continent. They were followed, around 600 CE, by a fleet dispatched by the Egyptian Pharaoh, Necho II, whose ships sailed along the continent's eastern seaboard.

But not until 2,000 years later, when Portuguese navigators and explorers set out in search of new lands – and a sea route to the Indies – did the continent begin to yield its secrets. In the fifteenth century, King John II of Portugal sent two expeditions under Diego Cão to Africa's western seaboard. History records that the explorer anchored south of what is now Namibia's Skeleton Coast and stepped ashore to set up a stone cross on top of a rocky cape. The cross stood for more than 400 years until the captain of a German vessel removed it late last century and took it to a museum in Berlin. Two years after Diego Cão left his cruciform,

Bartolomeu Dias, another Portuguese explorer, positioned a second cross in a bay he named Angra Pequena, Little Bay, now Lüderitz Bay.

Looking at the formidable dunes of the great Namib Desert as they tumble into the icy Atlantic, it is not difficult to understand why so few voyagers chose to venture inland. The oldest desert in the world – some eighty million years – the Namib seems denuded of life, scorched by noonday sun, cooled by chill night mists that billow in from the ocean shutting out the frosty moon. Yet, astonishingly, life exists above and below its surface as plants and creatures draw sustenance from the wind and moisture of its misty phantoms. Such life, from tiny beetles to mighty elephants, have made this improbable wilderness their home. Indeed, many species are found nowhere else in the world. Swept by searing winds, the highest dunes in the world – mountains of sand – roll across the desert like roaming clouds to meet at a place called Sossusvlei.

East of the Namib stand remnants of the time before man walked these lands: dinosaur tracks and petrified forests, the greatest meteorite on earth and ancient castles of clay. From the eroded cliffs of Fish River Canyon, through Namibia's quaint, colonial-style towns, to the wild expanses of Etosha and the Caprivi Strip, Namibia's brittle beauty is vast even by African standards. Yet, although four times the size of Britain, its population numbers fewer than one and a half million people, giving it one of the lowest population densities in the world, with fewer than two people to each square kilometre. This remarkably low number may ensure that the changes ravaging much of Africa never affect its latest republic.

Basking in summer temperatures – ranging from 10-33°C between October and April and from 6–26°C in winter between May and September – Namibia's unspoilt splendour makes it truly a land of the free, for the free. A developing network of well-maintained tar, gravel and dirt roads allows visitors to reach the farthest corners of what has been called Africa's Gem – from the fallen glory of the rocky Finger of God in the south to the majesty of the Okavango River and the rapids of the Popa Falls in the north; from the mystery of the White Lady of the Brandberg to the raw power of the Namib Desert; from the gigantic fossil woods of the Petrified Forest near Khorixas to the Hoba Meteorite near Grootfontein; from the abundant wildlife of that other Eden, Etosha National Park, to the fascination of the Skeleton Coast.

And its people, every bit as unique and colourful, include perhaps Africa's oldest race, the San Bushmen, whose affinity to the trackless desert and savannahs where they live seems almost miraculous. One of their legends underlines this unlikely symbiosis: 'Now you come, now you go. When you come again you will never go.'

The many African tribes and European settlers live in a country of contrasts and vibrant colour. It is bordered in the west by the mighty Atlantic whose shores are lined by the Namib-Naukluft Park, which sprawls across almost 50,000 square kilometres – an area larger than Denmark. The southern border with South Africa is formed by the Orange River. In the north, much of the border between Namibia and Angola is made up of the Kunene and Okavango Rivers. And to the east lies the Kalahari Desert which sweeps into Botswana.

Many contemporary aspects of Namibia bear witness to the Victorian age when the European powers carved up Africa. Even now, Herero women dress in Victorian fashions while the charming buildings of both Swakopmund and Windhoek, the capital, reflect nineteenth-century convention and style. These incongruous vestiges extend beyond costume or architecture to the national boundaries where two particular instances remain curious reminders of colonial days. The first is a narrow corridor of land, 482 kilometres long, extending as far as the Zambezi. The Caprivi Strip, so named after Baron von Caprivi, the German Chancellor of the time, is also known as the Devil's Finger. It was the outcome of the German Kaiser's ambition to join his western and eastern African empires together. The second anachronism, Walvis Bay, midway between the Kunene and Orange Rivers, was annexed in 1878 to become part of Britain's Cape Colony, yet it remained under South African jurisdiction until the end of 1994, when Namibia began to share in its administration.

Namibia forms three distinct topographical regions – the Namib Desert; the central inland plateau's mountains and plains with, most magnificent of all, Etosha National Park; and finally the Kalahari Desert in the south-east reaches of the country.

The Kalahari's western counterpart, the Namib Desert, stretches more than 2,000 kilometres along the African coast in an arid band between 150 and 200 kilometres wide. In these virtually waterless conditions, its unique animals and plants take their moisture from the cool mists that sweep in from the Atlantic.

The roving dunes along the southern tract of coast are older than any other in the world. To the north lies the legendary Skeleton Coast where the sun-bleached bones of sailors and whales lie side by side with rusting shipwrecks. There, the Namib's dunes are complemented by vast, hard-baked granite flats which stretch from one horizon to the next.

What little takes root in the way of vegetation must rank among the world's most unusual and enduring plants, chief of which is a remarkable dwarf tree that dates back to prehistoric times. Some existing specimens of the tree – *Welwitschia mirabilis* – are more than 2,000 years old. Other marvels have also adapted ingeniously to this cruel land and manage to survive the scorching daytime heat and freezing night temperatures.

Several rivers, most of them seasonal, flow westwards into the Atlantic along Namibia's long seaboard – from the northernmost Kunene River to the Orange River in the extreme south. Three major towns dominate the seaboard. In summertime, elegant Swakopmund, halfway between Angola and South Africa, is woken from its hibernation by masses of tourists who double its wintertime population. A little to the south, Walvis Bay, the deepest harbour on Africa's south-west coast, is another popular haven for tourists. The port serves freight and fishing vessels.

The port of Lüderitz, with its fairy-tale architecture, almost 500 kilometres south of Walvis Bay, has been in use since Bartolomeu Dias moored there in the fifteenth century. East of Walvis Bay, the Namib-Naukluft Park stretches far inland, culminating in dramatic 305-metre mountains of sand at Sossusvlei.

However, the most spectacular feature of the southern region is the deep cleft in the earth's surface, the Fish River Canyon, a colossal gorge more than 160 kilometres long.

On its eastern flank, the Namib Desert meets Namibia's immense inland plateau, the nation's second distinct topographical region, which forms the country's south-north backbone. This varies from brooding mountains with jagged 2,440-metre peaks to wide plains and sandy valleys. Amid the high mountains at Namibia's northernmost extremities, the Kunene and Okavango Rivers flow all year round, the latter feeding the Okavango Delta in neighbouring Botswana.

And it is there in the north, close to the Angolan border, that you find Namibia's most magical landscape – the wilderness wonderlands of Etosha National Park. One of the world's largest game parks, Etosha's 22,270 square kilometres – bigger than Wales – know no seasons. As day melts into night, so the weeks and months merge into one. The Etosha Pan, which gives the park its name, covers some 5,000 square kilometres in the east.

This dry pan used to be the lake into which the Kunene

River emptied itself, but following continental shifting, and the subsequent diversion of the Kunene's course to the Atlantic Ocean, the pan became what it is today. This immense shallow bowl, which fills only occasionally after the onset of the rains, is all that remains of that ancient lake. It is the source and sustenance of all life at Etosha, whose plains are home to a variety of creatures – birds, game animals and insects – some of which are found nowhere else in the world. As the scorching heat bakes the bleached and seemingly endless plains, these animals make their way to the rapidly dwindling waterholes in the pan to quench their thirst.

The land between Etosha and Windhoek, the capital city, is dotted with a host of small towns, such as Grootfontein and Otjiwarongo, where you can enjoy the distinctive charms of Namibian society. The most densely populated region of Namibia is Owambo, where the great majority of people live in rural settings.

Windhoek lies almost at the centre of Namibia, linked to the main urban areas and neighbouring countries by an extensive and expanding infrastructure.

The capital's charm – buildings of colonial German design, and modern skyscrapers – is enhanced by its location close to the Auas and Eros Mountains and not far from the Khomas Hochland in the west.

East of Windhoek, the boundless Kalahari Desert, which stretches southwards down the country's eastern flank straddling the border with Botswana, forms Namibia's third distinct landscape, surprisingly different from its western counterpart. For, unlike the Namib, the Kalahari is comparatively rich in plants and grasses, and sustains a great variety of life. Camel-thorn, red ebony and silver terminalia trees mix with a wide range of shrubs and succulents, providing welcome shade and refreshment for the people and creatures that live in the desert.

Keetmanshoop, the largest town at the edge of the Kalahari, grew up in the south around a mission station which later became a German military garrison.

Long before the Europeans first sailed along Africa's south-west coast, Namibia's people enjoyed their ancient ways and age-old beliefs following a destiny diverted only by the first footsteps of Western navigators, explorers, missionaries and carpet-baggers.

Belonging to eleven groups, a rich tapestry of tribes and people has endowed Namibia with its striking and varied cultural legacy. These myriad people have become as one in their new-found freedom. Yet each group retains a distinctive character and language, setting it apart from its neighbours.

Under the old, pre-independence South African administration, these cultures were demarcated geographically by a series of ethnic 'homelands' – such as Koakoland, Owambo, Kavango, Bushmanland, Hereroland and Damaraland. But these were swept away in 1990 by a new local government structure that divided Namibia into thirteen regional authorities, each with its own political constituencies.

Almost one-tenth of Namibia's people, many of them European, make their home in Windhoek. In the few years since independence, the pace of migration from rural areas into the towns and city, spurred by the relentless drought that ravaged southern Africa at the end of the 1980s and in the early 1990s, quickened. Peasants, labourers and village folk flocked to the capital in search of jobs and food.

Namibia's original citizens, long before the other groups migrated to the south-west of the continent, are the San Bushmen. They once occupied the whole of southern Africa; their language is similar to that of their South African kith and kin, the Nama. Fine-boned and lightly coloured, these hunter gatherers, a nomadic people skilled in bushcraft and survival in the harshest conditions, are thought to have roamed Namibia's wildernesses thousands of years ago. Their rock paintings, in caves and on cliffs throughout the country, depict San life, hunting, and the animals around them. For centuries they roamed free, at peace with nature. It was only when they came in contact with outside influences that disaster struck – with the influx of Nama pastoralists, themselves descendants of the Khoikhoi of the Cape Province. This invasion during the early eighteenth century was a tragedy for these peaceful people – and it was compounded when the Wambo and Damara tribes swept in behind the Nama, while the Bantu-speaking Herero filtered into the Kaokoveld in north-west Namibia, before moving through the centre of the country.

Finally large numbers of the Oorlam tribe, themselves Nama who had closer contact with Western influences in the Cape, advanced into Namibia's heartlands. They brought with them weapons as well as a form of the Dutch language from the European communities in southern Africa. This dialect later became Afrikaans, which is still spoken widely in Namibia. It allows communication between indigenous tribes found in the country. Many customs and traditions have been devastated and Namibia's extraordinary cultural heritage is now under threat from modernization and development. But a few remain, as yet untrammelled by Western influence, thus preserving the country's unique legacy.

Namibia has about 70,000 European citizens, most of whom speak Afrikaans, while others are mainly of German or English descent.

The Wambo tribe's 800,000 people, the largest single group, live in the region between Etosha and Angola. To the north-east, Okavango is home to the 180,000 people of the Kavango tribe, the second largest group. Three tribes – the Herero, Himba and Mbanderu – form the 90,000 people of what was Hereroland in Otjozondjupa, which lies to the south of Okavango. During German rule the Herero were almost decimated. Many now roam Windhoek and other towns selling trinkets, or surviving how they can.

The home of the Tjimba and Himba tribes, who are related to the Herero, was Kaokoveld in Kunene. Scorning materialism and the trappings of modern civilization, much like the Maasai of East Africa, the Himba have become a fascination for Western observers intrigued by their traditional way of life. They were forced into their empty wastelands during the last century by the Nama tribe.

Erongo – where the Damara people endure a harsh

existence – is part of the old Damaraland. It is thought the Damara travelled southwards from western Africa through the centre of the continent in a migration lasting many centuries, bringing with them the secrets of extracting iron and making pottery.

The homelands of the Nama lie in the south in Karas, an area dominated by the Orange River. Until the end of the eighteenth century the Nama were at peace. But that was shattered by a massive influx of Herero in search of grazing. The war between the Herero and the Nama lasted for decades and claimed thousands of victims. The most tragic of all Western influences were the firearms brought in by the bellicose Oorlam who propelled South West Africa into an era of unprecedented confrontation. The mixed-race Baster people were driven northwards by the Boers in the 1860s across the Orange River to settle south of what is now Windhoek in the Hardap Region. These protracted migrations over vast areas laid the foundations for today's Namibian cultures. But it was a period characterized by open warfare as tribes found themselves competing for land and scarce resources. Whole generations perished but little was accomplished, except to consolidate the colonialist stranglehold over the land and its people.

Namibia's long history is also stained with the bloodshed from white domination – a tide of terror and belligerence that may never be erased entirely from Namibian soil.

Even before the nineteenth century, Europe's superpowers vied for supremacy of south-western Africa's strategic bays and inlets. To thwart other roving European forces seeking to expand their control of Africa's western flank, the Dutch seized Walvis Bay and Lüderitz Bay in 1793. But when the British took control of the Cape of Good Hope two years later, they also took possession of Walvis Bay and a string of other key locations.

Few Europeans, if any, ventured into the heart of Namibia – it was far too dangerous. The great quests came with the onset of the nineteenth century. The first sorties into Namibia's interior were made by a small corps of hardy explorers, such as Pieter Pienaar who ventured inland by way of rivers like the Swakop. It was not until the arrival of the missionaries, however, that the first major expeditions were accomplished. Among the many Christian pioneers, the names of Abraham and Christian Albrecht, who lived with the Nama and stopped at nothing to spread their faith, ring loudest. Johann Heinrich Schmelen, another Christian missionary, was an extraordinary man who took a Nama bride and set her to work translating the Bible into Nama. The London Missionary Society focused on what is now the Caprivi Strip where the most famous of all missionaries, David Livingstone, was stationed between 1850 and 1851. All across Namibia missionaries spread the word, settling among the Nama, Herero, Wambo and other tribes.

But the Christian message did nothing to prevent the conflicts which marred the final years of the last century. British attempts to end inter-tribal rivalry were feeble, mainly because they had no wish to become enmeshed. And when Adolf Lüderitz, a trader from Bremen, appealed to the Kaiser to do something in 1882, Bismarck decided to act. He annexed the whole of what is now Namibia, except for Walvis Bay and some small islands which the British retained.

At first the small German colonial administration operated a policy of *laissez-faire*. But as the bloodshed between tribes continued, the Germans cut supplies of arms and ammunition, built forts and brought in a military corps, the Schutztruppe. In 1904 these cold-blooded killers instigated a reign of terror in which most of the 80,000-strong Herero men, women and children were slaughtered. By the end of 1907 the tribe counted their numbers in hundreds.

This ethnic slaughter preceded the discovery of a rich diamond field by railway worker Zacharias Lewala, a former miner from South Africa's Kimberley diamond mines. One day, in April 1908, he was shovelling drifting sand from the line near Grasplatz Station, when he noticed the telltale twinkle of a diamond. Lewala scooped up the glistening stone and gave it to his boss, August Stauch, a German railway inspector. Stauch immediately staked a claim to that piece of desert. It came to be called Kolmanskop. The news spread like wildfire and, within weeks, dozens of prospectors had pegged out the entire area south-east of Lüderitz. De Beers, the great South African diamond conglomerate, eager to protect its markets, played down suggestions that the deposits were worth anything, while the colonial administration gave mining concessions only to German syndicates. Prisoners of war from the Herero rebellion were used as slave labour, since there were no other Africans in the diamond zone. Diamond fever continued and new fields were constantly being discovered, particularly in the first two decades of the century. Driven by diamond wealth, the colony's economy grew swiftly. Business expanded and roads, railways and port facilities developed. By 1913, one-fifth of all Africa's mined diamonds came from Namibia.

But at the height of this unparalleled prosperity, German South West Africa became embroiled in World War I. Isolated from the German empire, far from any defensive resources, it was at the mercy of the British forces. But South Africa delayed the push into German South West Africa until the 1914 Boer rebellion was quelled.

Then, in January 1915, South African forces – under the British flag – landed at Swakopmund and Lüderitz. Vastly outnumbered, the Germans surrendered within six months – on 9 July 1915. It was the first German colony to be captured by British forces and a new administration was installed at Windhoek.

But the change did nothing to lift the burden of oppression. Indeed it signalled yet another chapter in the colony's long history of suffering, one that lasted more than seven decades.

In 1919, under the newly formed League of Nations, South West Africa, as Namibia now became known, was entrusted to South Africa as a mandated territory. The League's intentions could not be doubted. It prohibited South Africa from conscripting Africans into military service, and indeed ordered the trustees to advance the country's social and economic status. But the mandate failed to spell out the need for eventual self-government and this crucial omission allowed South Africa to treat the country as its own colony. In effect this permitted South Africa to plunder its resources and exploit its people. The interests of white South Africans were ever first, and the riches too good to miss. In 1920, Ernest Oppenheimer snapped up the diamond concessions from the nine German companies that operated the syndicate. He paid the bargain price of forty million marks and founded Consolidated Diamond Mines – CDM. In the first twelve years of mining, six and a half million carats of diamonds – a carat is 200 milligrams – were recovered.

Land was wealth, too, and now the Afrikaner settlers threw the peasants off the land to carve out farms on the rich grazing lands of the central plateau. Six years after the war ended, the white population had doubled. By 1926, the indigenous occupiers of their native pastures had been forced out to make way for almost 1,000 white farms, each averaging about 37,000 acres. These reluctant itinerants were destined to wander semi-desert regions seeking pastures for their herds. Under apartheid, black and mixed-race people were forced to live away from white communities. Pretoria established a commission to map out tribal homelands. Known as the Odendaal Plan, after the commission's chairman, it divided the various tribes to prevent them from rebellion and insurgency. Homelands such as Kavango, Owambo and Damaraland were created in the overgrazed and overpopulated regions of Namibia, mainly in the northern wilderness. Residents could only leave if they found work in a white area under a white master.

Freedom for much of the rest of Africa dawned in the 1960s, however, and these new nations changed the balance of power within the United Nations. Their pressure put Namibia's plight on the world agenda. And, in October 1966, the United Nations ended the South African mandate, assuming responsibility for South West Africa under the United Nations Council for Namibia. But South Africa, which accused the UN of acting illegally, refused to relinquish power, sparking off a general strike and rebellions. South Africa responded with a state emergency and imposed virtual martial law.

At the start of the 1970s, the UN recognized the South West African People's Organization (SWAPO) as 'the sole and authentic representative of the Namibian people'. Under Shafiishuna Samuel Nujoma, SWAPO set out to unite all Namibians. Still South Africa refused to loosen its stranglehold.

It was Portugal's eventual departure from Africa as a colonial power in 1975 that acted as the real catalyst for freedom, giving SWAPO a platform in Angola from which to transform its insurrections into a full military offensive. Now Namibia's northern border provided sanctuary for SWAPO's guerrilla arm – the People's Liberation Army of Namibia (PLAN). South Africa labelled SWAPO as a communist organization, as most international support for SWAPO came from communist and Scandinavian countries. As a result, South Africa began a campaign of terror in northern Namibia, and thousands of refugees fled to Angola, Botswana and Zambia. Many of these exiles were recruited by PLAN, strengthening the fight for freedom. SWAPO broadened its political support within Namibia by forging alliances with other political groups, and winning the support of the churches. By the late 1970s, SWAPO was truly national, representing a complete cross-section of Namibian society. But in 1978 South Africa staged unrepresentative elections in Windhoek, which were immediately condemned as a 'sham' by the United Nations.

To combat the thousands of troops that South Africa poured into northern Namibia, SWAPO needed a cohesive military strategy and coordinated initiatives. Roads were mined, ambushes laid and military bases raided.

The liberation war reached its height in the 1980s. Intense fighting in densely populated Owambo spread rapidly to Kavango and the barren Kaoko. PLAN also carried the war to other areas, including the central and southern regions – even Windhoek itself.

PLAN's spy-ring was extraordinarily skilled; the freedom fighters were given food, water, shelter and vital information, allowing raids to have the maximum impact. At the same time, South Africa was able to infiltrate PLAN with spies of its own. SWAPO's discovery of this fact led to many innocent people being accused of spying for the enemy. As a result, South African military operations became increasingly brutal. Namibians were press-ganged into uniform and forced to take up arms against their own kin – while specialized terror units, Koevoets, were sent into battle.

The war drained South Africa of billions of rands – and

its enthusiasm for the fight. This war of thirty years, labelled by one side as a liberation struggle, and by the other as the attempted infiltration of communism, reached a stalemate. Neither side could win, and it became clear other means of ending this conflict had to be found.

The 1988 agreement, which the Americans brokered between South Africa and Cuba to end the war in Angola, opened the door for Namibia's independence. Almost 50,000 refugees, the most distinguished of these being Samuel Nujoma himself, flooded back into the country for the November 1989 elections. The turnout was almost 100 per cent. SWAPO won a clear majority with 57.3 per cent of the vote, giving them forty-one of the seventy-two seats in Namibia's fledging parliament. They and the six other parties soon agreed on the constitution. Freedom for all – in religion, association, speech, thought and print – was guaranteed, and all discrimination outlawed.

Finally, on the night of 21 March 1990, after a struggle that had lasted well over a century, thousands of Namibians watched as the proud flag of their new nation was unfurled for the first time. And in the presence of UN Secretary General Javier Perez de Cuellar and world leaders, Sam Nujoma became the first President of Namibia.

From: *Journey Through Namibia*

# Jungle

JOSEPH CONRAD WAS at one time a steamer captain on the River Congo, an experience he drew on to breathe life into his novel, *Heart of Darkness.*

A century after his expeditions in the seething jungles of central Africa, I was first introduced to the rain forests of the same region, while exploring the eastern flank of what was then the dictatorship of Zaire.

Over the decades I've roamed the world, I've found myself time and again in both jungle and cloud forest. Zigzagging routes through equatorial Africa, Latin America and the Far East, Conrad's writing has inspired me in a base and primitive way.

On every expedition, he, his characters, and I, have been trussed up together in an unlikely fraternity – each one of us an outsider in a landscape we neither knew nor understood. We shared the same sense of anguish and trepidation, questioning what we were doing in a realm gravely at odds with our own.

Early one evening at Manaus, the sprawling Brazilian city founded on the short-lived nineteenth-century rubber boom, I was standing on the boardwalk, staring out at the Amazon's sea-like expanse, marvelling at it. Conrad's description of Marlow's cursed journey up the Congo rang out in my head, as I wondered how I would ever be able to match the genius of past generations.

Standing there, with the sound of the jungle feasting on itself, I was approached by a boy of about twelve. Like so many Brazilian kids his age, he was hustling – offering to shine shoes, run errands, or provide the inside story to foreigners stupid enough to be robbed – as I had been that very morning.

'Shoe shine, señor?'

'No thanks.'

'Cigarette?'

'No. Don't smoke.'

'Nice girl?'

I balked.

'*No!*'

'Information?'

'What information?'

'Survival information.'

Panning down from the river, I looked at the hustler's face. It was shiny and angelic, tinged golden yellow in the last strains of dusk.

'What line in survival information are you offering?'

'Jungle survival, señor.'

'D'you know the jungle?'

'*Sí*, I am from the jungle.'

'Then what are you doing here in Manaus?'

The boy pulled a worn old brush from either pocket and held them up.

'Shining shoes,' he said.

'How much is the information on offer... the jungle survival information?'

The boy bit his lower lip, stuffed away his brushes, and said:

'The price of a bowl of soup, and a piece of bread.'

'You've got a deal.'

Retreating from the boardwalk's vantage point, we slipped into the long shadows where the subculture of bars was stirring to life.

'I am Miguel,' said the boy, taking a seat on a battered chair.

I introduced myself, adding:

'I've got high hopes for you.'

Miguel ordered a bowl of meat soup, and a chunk of bread.

When the food had been served and devoured, he wiped a hand over his mouth, burped, thanked me, then God, and cleared his throat:

'City people like you die in the jungle,' he said coldly.

'That's why guys like me need survival information – the kind you promised to provide in return for the agreed fee.'

'Good soup,' the boy said, wiping his mouth again.

'So, what's the survival information?'

Miguel, the shoe-shine boy and all-round informant, thought hard.

'The way to survive in the jungle is not to be frightened of it,' he explained. 'Don't stand against it, but go with its flow… like a branch being carried downstream.'

'How did you know I was frightened?'

'I can see it in your face, señor.'

'*Really*? Is it that obvious?'

Miguel nodded fast.

'And being frightened like you are means the jungle will

eat you up,' he said. 'Everyone knows that the jungle can smell frightened people.'

'Do you have any other tips?'

'Yes.'

'What?'

'You should rub Vicks VapoRub on your ankles at night.'

'Why?'

'Because it keeps the mosquitos away.'

'Anything else?'

'Always carry a sharp knife.'

'For killing wild animals when they attack me?'

'*No!*' Miguel exclaimed. 'Not for that.'

'Then, what for?'

'For killing yourself when you can't stand the jungle anymore.'

From: *Jungle: The Anthologies*

## Legends of the Fire Spirits

THE OCCIDENT HAS never found it easy to grasp the strange netherworld of spirits that followers of Islam universally believe exist in a realm overlaying our own.

Although descended from an Oriental family with its roots in the mountain fortress of Afghanistan's Hindu Kush, I had been born and brought up in the West. I thought I knew the East. After all, I was well accustomed from childhood to understanding the finer points of Arab etiquette, and I had been taught its tales, gleaned from *Alf Layla wa Layla – A Thousand and One Nights.*

That fabulous treasury of stories had introduced me early on to the extraordinary possibilities of a world peopled by invisible legions of jinn. So when we came to live at Dar Khalifa, the Caliph's House, I felt as if nothing could surprise me.

How wrong I was.

From the first moment that we crossed the threshold, I realized that I was way out of my depth. The house had been empty for almost a decade. Whereas in the West an empty home might appeal to squatters, in the East there is a danger of quite a different kind. The unlawful occupants of our new home were not human, but superhuman.

The guardians who came with the property, as if through some medieval rights sale, warned us from the outset that there was extreme danger all around. When I declared that we would be moving into the house right away to supervise the renovations, they laughed nervously – until, that is, they realized I was serious. Terrified, contorted expressions then swept across their faces, and they begged us to leave post-haste.

The jinn would not take kindly to intruders, they told me. For in the years that the house had been empty, it had become their home. Dare to trespass and they might kill us, the leader of the guardians declared. Irritated, yet willing to go along with them for the sake of respecting local sensitivities, I asked what to do. The chief guardian, whose name was Osman, swept his arms out wide, and yelled: 'You must hold an exorcism!'

Back in London I would have had no idea where to find an exorcist, let alone a troop of them. But Morocco is very different. It may be perched in Africa's north-west corner, just eight miles from the gates of Europe, but in many ways it is the deepest, darkest Orient.

And that is what is so appealing about it.

I asked around and, very soon, found myself in the old imperial city of Meknès. According to all my informants it was the centre of exorcists. And they were right. A few minutes after my arrival I was offered dozens of exorcists from the Aissawa brotherhood. I negotiated a price for twenty, and the exorcist dealer threw in a further four of them for free. The only catch was that I was obliged to pay in advance.

A day or so later I arrived home and was greeted by the guardians' long looks. The jinn were already exacting their revenge, they told me. A dead cat had been found in the garden with its head cut off. A tree had fallen in the wind and broken a window. And the maid, hired to look after our baby son, had run off screaming for no reason at all. I held out a hand at arm's length and whispered confidently, 'Have no fear, the exorcists are coming.'

The guardians perked up.

They asked when exactly the visitors would arrive.

I shrugged.

'They'll come when they are ready,' I said.

My wife insisted I was mad to have handed over wads of money to exorcists I didn't know. She said she could hear them all the way in Meknès, howling with laughter.

A day passed, then another.

I kicked myself at having been so ingenuous as to pay in advance. But then at that moment I heard the wild, whooping sound of men in high spirits, against a backdrop of grinding noise. A huge cement truck was inching its way down our lane. On the back were riding the exorcists, as if on some infernal chariot. I pointed at them and grinned, and the guardians grinned too.

Through days and nights the Aissawa wreaked their terrible work.

They slaughtered and skinned a goat at what they said was the heart of the house. As the person obliged to purchase the animal, I found myself naturally interested in how its execution would feature in the cleansing of my home of supernatural elements. When stripped of its skin, the carcass was beheaded, and its gallbladder swallowed by one of the group. The others slit open its belly and rifled through the organs, which gleamed like jewels in the candlelight.

One of the Aissawa then poured milk in all corners of the house, and another did the same with blood. Drums beat, and high-pitched homemade oboes wailed. The drumming grew faster and faster as the night wore on. And as it did so, the exorcists stepped into another plane, a kind of twilight zone of their own imagination.

They cut their wrists with knives and drank their own blood, then collapsed on the ground in a trance. Yet more massed in a dark, damp room at the far end of the house. They barricaded themselves inside, killed chickens and drank more blood.

And all the while the drums beat and the oboes shrieked. I wondered if the walls would tumble down as they had done in Jericho.

I whispered sternly to the Aissawa leader that they could leave. He laughed, a wild hearty laugh, and I swear his eyes flashed red with fire. He would only quit our home, he said, when the jinn had been sucked out of the walls and swallowed. I explained that my wife was growing impatient, and was uncomfortable at having the walls and floor strewn with freshly purged blood. The leader of the exorcists caught my glance in his. Widening his eyes in the most terrifying manner, he told me that he had never been in a house so consumed with evil spirits.

Then he asked for more money, and for another goat.

The next day, after brokering a deal which involved a handful of crisp hundred-dirham notes, the exorcists clambered aboard the cement truck. They rolled back down the lane and through the shantytown to the open road. My wife gave me one of those looks that instilled pure fear. I bragged out loud that the house was now squeaky clean, that the last thing we ever needed to worry about again were jinn.

In the years since, I have found myself living in a country where the belief in these normally invisible spirits is complete and unshakable. Jinn are described in the Qur'an, and they are a part of life for all God-fearing Muslims in Morocco and across the Islamic world. The Qur'an tells us that when God created Man from clay, he created a second race of beings – jinn – from 'smokeless fire'. Jinn are not ghosts, that is they are not spirits of the dead. Far from it. They are living entities just like us. They are born, get married, and die just like humans. Some are good and others bad, some ugly, while others are radiantly beautiful.

Indeed, there are many tales of mortal men being wooed by the charms of voluptuous women, only to realize later that they are not human, but jinn. The difference between us and them is that they have magical powers, and can decide when to be visible and when not. They can fly through the air, change their form, and are capable of magical feats of the most extraordinary kind.

The nineteenth century's fascination with *The Arabian Nights* saw the deeds and misdeeds of jinn enter Victorian drawing-rooms. The creatures slipped into Western communal folklore through the tales of Aladdin, Sindbad and others, mixed in with epic quests, treasure, flying carpets and enchanted lands. And through the endless adaptations for children, and all the Hollywood renditions, jinn became known to us all.

But gone was the Oriental imagery – the sly, ferocious race that lives among us, replaced by a comic jumble of towering yet quite loveable creatures, who go by the name of 'genies'.

Anyone who's spent any time in the Arab world knows the difference between Hollywood's depiction and that which is found embedded deep in local culture.

Living in a country like Morocco, where belief in jinn is all-pervasive, provides situations such as the ones we faced at the Caliph's House. It brings an extraordinary level of cultural possibility that simply doesn't exist in the Occidental world. Imagine it: that all around you there may be invisible spirits, sitting, standing, laughing, chatting, cackling, crouching on the floor. Some of them are minute, while others tower hundreds of feet into the air. The more you think about it, and live with it, the more appealing the idea of jinn becomes. And the longer you live in a place where everyone believes, the more you find yourself believing, too.

Long before I moved to Morocco, I had searched for a readable book about jinn and their world. But there wasn't one. When I asked friends who were scholars in Islamic culture and tradition, they recommended barely readable texts written by academics for academics. Years passed. Then, through a kind of magic that was from the realm of jinn themselves, Robert Lebling contacted me out of the blue. He spoke of a work, a great labour of love, which would reveal to the West all it needed to know about jinn.

My prayers had been answered.

The boundaries of Lebling's work surpassed my wildest dreams. The book's scope exceeds simply listing stories of jinn taken from Islamic texts and Arab folklore.

Lebling has left no stone unturned in his enquiry, roaming through traditional Eastern literature as well as the modern media, in search of anything which gives us a better understanding of jinn and their world. The result is a truly extraordinary masterwork, a treasury within itself that can be consulted at random, dipped into as a bedside book, or read from cover to cover in a fabulous feast for the imagination and the enquiring mind.

Through its pages, we learn that the belief in jinn is certainly pre-Islamic, and that there are various distinct forms of these creatures. The Qur'an devotes an entire Sura to them, a form of life that is inextricably linked to the cultural and religious tapestry of Arab and Islamic lands.

Lebling details clearly how followers of Islam perceive the realm of jinn, what the Prophet Mohammed said about them, and how regional and geographic divide has shaped them within local culture. An entire section is devoted to the study and appreciation of jinn by geographic location – through Morocco, Tunisia and Egypt, to Arabia and Palestine, Turkey, Iraq and Iran; as well as through Nigeria, Malaysia, Zanzibar and beyond.

We learn that the Arabic word for 'crazy' – *majnun* – comes from the same root as the word 'jinn', suggesting that a deranged person is possessed in some way. And that jinn are believed to lurk in wells and lavatories, in addition to their haunting empty buildings, such as our home. Space is given to King Solomon, the one human who could control jinn through the magical ring he wore.

And Lebling describes the extraordinary encounters between those of us created from clay and the others, shaped from smokeless fire. These include examples of humans whom have married jinn unwittingly, and others such as the fourteenth-century Moroccan magician, Muhammad ibn al-Hajj al-Tilimsani, whose work *Suns of Lights and Treasures of Secrets*, provides a spell for anyone wishing to seduce the daughter of the White King of the jinn.

*Legends of the Fire Spirits* provides a transparent window into Arab and Islamic society that is more usually clouded over, opaque to all except Arabists and scholars of Islam. The subject is one known to Muslims, embracing a belief that stands at the heart of the Islamic faith, but one that until now has been largely misrepresented and misunderstood in the West.

As for life at the Caliph's House, all is not well.

One of the guardians recently almost severed his hand while sharpening an axe in the garden. Then, last week, the maid tripped and cut her foot badly, and on the same day the swimming pool turned an eerie shade of yellowy green.

The guardians have been imploring me to hold another exorcism. The very thought of it fills me with anxiety. Most of all, I don't know how I'll break it to my wife. But, as all my friends assure me, everyone knows that even the best exorcism has to be renewed once in a while.

From: *Legends of the Fire Spirits*

## Marrakech: The Red City

SIX DAYS AGO I saw a man sitting in J'ma al Fna, the vast central square of Marrakech.

He was bald, with a long, tatty beard and a single silver earring reflecting the light. I knew he wasn't a Moroccan because of the look in his eye. He looked as if he had seen a miracle. I was waiting for a friend to turn up and we got talking. The man was a German called Casper. He told me he had travelled for sixteen years. It seemed to him that every inch of the world had passed beneath his feet. Sapphire eyes wide with wonder, hands out, fingers splayed, he told me that every minute until then had been the preparation – the preparation for that sight.

'This is the world,' he said in a soft Bavarian voice.

I asked him what he meant. He smiled.

'You don't feel it?'

I didn't reply.

'You don't feel it?' he repeated.

'What? Feel what?'

'The humanity,' he said.

Casper stood to his feet and staggered away, mumbling something about a drink of cold water. Then he was gone. I stood there, gazing out at the square's stew of human life – snake handlers and fortune-tellers, healers and madmen, door-to-door dentists, witches, water-sellers, and a single blind man waiting for a coin to be pressed into his palm. Casper from Bavaria was right. There is perhaps no spot on earth so alive, so human, as J'ma al Fna, the 'Place of

Execution'.

Like almost everyone else who has ever been there, I have tried to understand Marrakech. I have sat in Argana, my favourite café overlooking the square, and I have watched, listened, and pondered. Is it Africa? Is it Morocco? Is it a tourist destination *par excellence?* Or is it a strange kind of paradise, a paradise for the senses? The answer is that Marrakech is all of these things, and a great deal more.

My only grumble is that these days the Red City is far too easy to reach.

You fly in, and half an hour later you can be embedded in the medina or lazing by a pool, wondering where on earth you are. Look at the map. Study it, and you see that you are deep in the desert, with the Atlas Mountains rising up behind you. If I had my way, you would still have to struggle to get to Marrakech – to really earn it, like every other traveller in history.

For there's nothing like perspiration to make one appreciative.

With the afternoon heat too suffocating in the square, the light too bright for any but a Marrachi's eyes, I slipped into the labyrinth of the medina.

Cool vaulted stone, courtyards latticed with bamboo staves, casting zebra stripes across the merchants and their stalls. What an emporium – mountains of turmeric, paprika, salted almonds and dates, yellow leather slippers laid out in rows, ostrich eggs and incense, chameleons in wire cages, and beef tenderloins nestled on fragrant beds of mint.

Roam the medina's narrow passages and you are dragged back in time. Marrakech may be prosperous these days, bolstered by tourist wealth, but the medina is still intact, vibrant, raging with life, as it's been for centuries. There may be Chinese plastic dolls on offer, and second-hand TVs stacked up by the dozen, and racks of mobile phones, but don't be deceived. Marrakech moves on an ancient rhythm. The decoration comes and goes, as do the wares, but the soul does not alter.

Of all the stalls and shops, there is one that I visit on every journey to the Red City. It is the Maison de Meknès, a low-fronted place, on a side-street off a side-street. There are steps going down, rounded by decades of eager feet. Inside, the ceiling is low, cobwebbed, and the shelves beneath it cluttered with treasure. There are ancient Berber chests, silver teapots, ebony footstools, and swords once used by warring tribes, and cartons of postcards left by the French, box Brownie cameras, candlesticks, silk wedding belts, and camel headdresses crafted from indigo wool.

The proprietor is a smug-faced man with tobacco-coloured eyes called Omar bin Mohammed. He is always perched on a stool behind a pool of light just inside the door. You don't see him at first, not until your eyes have become accustomed to the darkness. Omar is greedy for business, but there is one thing that he enjoys more than loading tourists up with loot. He loves to tell stories. Visit his shop and you can't leave until you have sat awhile on a low, leather-topped stool, quaffed a glass of boiling mint tea, and listened.

The first time I stepped into the shop was to ask for directions. It was early in the morning, before the crowds of tourists had begun to ramble through. None of the other emporia were open, and Omar was still only preparing, washing the steps leading down into his lair. I had asked him the way to the main square. Before I knew it I had been lured inside. I spent all day in there, listening. The first thing Omar told me when I crossed the threshold was that nothing – absolutely nothing – was for sale. However much I wanted one of the ancient Berber boxes, or the rough Saharan shields, or the amber necklaces, I was out of luck, he said.

'Is it a museum, then?' I asked.

Omar bin Mohammed clawed a hand through the scrub of grey beard on his cheek.

'My shop isn't like the others in the medina,' he hissed. 'The others, they're charlatans. They'll eat you up, sell you their mothers.'

'Then how is your place different? Is your merchandise of higher quality?'

Omar blew his nose into an oversized handkerchief, and rubbed his thumbs to his eyes.

'No, no,' he said. 'All this stuff I'm selling is worthless. It may look nice to you, because you don't know. The light's bad in here. An empty tin can would look like treasure in this light. Take something away and the first time you'd realize it's rubbish is when you are home.'

'I really don't understand why you're telling me this.'

Omar held his right palm out in the air.

'There's a problem,' he said. 'I have endured it since my youth.'

I wondered what the shopkeeper was talking about. People I've just met are always offloading their troubles on me. I braced myself to be petitioned for charity.

'We all have problems,' I said.

'You understand,' came the reply. 'And my problem is that I can't help but tell the truth.'

'That doesn't sound like a problem. Quite the opposite in fact.'

Omar the shopkeeper blinked hard.

'You have no idea. When you're a salesman here in the Marrakech medina, lying is the first thing you learn. Generation after generation, they pass it on. It's the secret ingredient, the frame for a salesman's life. Lie well and you can make a fortune every day. Only then will your wife be happy, only then will your children walk with pride.'

'Can't you just pretend to lie?'

'That's it,' said Omar. 'The other shopkeepers say I'm a fool, that I should simply trick the tourists like everyone else. After all most of them will never be back. And what are tourists for but for tricking?'

'*So?*'

'So in my shop nothing's for sale.'

'Ah,' I said.

Omar paused, flexed his neck, and smiled.

'Nothing's for sale...' he repeated. 'Instead, it's all free. Absolutely free!'

I looked greedily at the shelves. One of the ancient Berber

coffers had caught my eye. The thought of getting it for nothing was suddenly very pleasing.

'Can I have that, then?'

'Of course you can,' said Omar.

'Without charge? Can I just take it?'

'I told you,' he said, 'I give the objects away.'

'I'm so glad I came inside here.'

'I'm glad you did, too,' said the shopkeeper.

I stood up and moved over to the Berber chest. Omar encouraged me to pull back the lid, revealing a felt-trimmed interior.

'Oh, there's something I should tell you,' he said gently.

'What?'

'That to every item in here there's something attached.'

Again, I didn't quite understand.

'What's that?'

'A story.'

I glanced over at the shopkeeper and narrowed my eyes.

'Huh?'

'If you want to take an item,' he said, 'then you have to buy the story attached to it.'

Omar blinked. Then I blinked. He rubbed a hand to his face again, and I pondered the arrangement. In a city where competition for tourist dollars had reached fever pitch, Omar bin Mohammed had come up with a ruse like none other. He grinned hard, then tried to look meek.

'What story is attached to that chest?'

'It's called "The Horseman and the Snake".'

'How much does it cost to hear it?'

'Six hundred dirhams.'

'That's forty pounds,' I said. 'That chest isn't worth that.'

'I told you, the objects I'm giving away are not special at all. The chest looks nice but it's worthless.'

'Then why should I fork out six hundred dirhams for something of such little value?'

Omar bin Mohammed wove his fingers together and bowed them towards the floor.

'For the story,' he said.

I pulled out three high-denomination bills.

'Here's the money.'

A moment later the bills had been tucked beneath layers of clothing, and the Berber chest had been wrapped in newspaper.

'It's a good choice,' said Omar.

'But I thought you said you were dealing in rubbish.'

'That chest may be rubbish,' he said, 'but "The Horseman and the Snake" is worth three times the money I'm charging you for it.'

Leaning back on his stool, Omar bin Mohammed stared hard into the pool of light just inside his door, and he began:

'Once upon a time,' he said, 'long ago and many days travel from where we sit, there was a kingdom called the Land of Pots and Pans. Everyone there was happy, and everyone was prosperous, made so by their thriving business of selling pots and pans to the other kingdoms all around.'

Omar the salesman paused to pass me a glass of sweet mint tea.

'Now,' he said, 'in the Land of Pots and Pans there were

all sorts of animals, except for snakes. No one had ever seen a snake, and no one had ever imagined such a creature. One day a woodcutter was asleep in the forest, when a long, green serpent slithered up to him and slid into his open mouth and down his throat. The woodcutter woke up, as the snake suffocated him. Panicking, he managed to stand up and flap his arms all around, moaning as loudly as he could.

'As luck would have it, a horseman was riding by at that precise moment. He saw the woodcutter waving his arms in distress. Having come from the neighbouring land where snakes were plentiful, he realized immediately what had happened. Pulling out his whip, he leapt from his steed and began to whip the poor woodcutter's stomach with all his strength.

'The woodcutter tried to protest, but half-suffocated by the serpent and wounded from the horseman's seemingly unprovoked attack, he could do nothing except fall to his knees. Displeased at the discomfort of its hiding place, the snake reversed up out of the woodcutter's throat and slithered away. Seeing this, the horseman jumped back onto his mount and rode off without a word. Hailing from a land where such attacks were frequent, he didn't give the matter another thought. As he caught his breath, the woodcutter began to understand what had happened, and that the horseman had attacked him in silence because time was of the essence, before the reptile had injected venom into his bloodstream.'

Omar bin Mohammed held up the Berber chest wrapped in newspaper and grinned.

154

'Don't forget the story,' he said. 'You will appreciate it all the more because you have paid to hear it. Allow it to move around your head, the more it does so, the more its real value will become apparent.'

These days Marrakech seems to be charging ahead, like a stagecoach hurtling into the night.

I can think of few places that are quite so alive, quite so popular. There are people everywhere, all of them doing something, selling something, or waiting for something to happen. In most other cities the combination would be asphyxiating, but not in Marrakech. I think it's because everyone living in or visiting the city understands that they are there at a particular time. There's a sense that the cocktail of life is just right, that it's something which occurs very seldom.

For centuries Marrakech has been a remote staging post, a frontier before the desert. The intrepid have passed through en route south into the Sahara, or eastwards towards Mecca. It has always been a caravanserai, where possessions have been bought and sold, and stories swapped: a place where people live on the edge, thankful that they are there.

As I stroll through the central square of J'ma al Fna, I often find myself pondering how Marrakech has become what it has – the world's most celebrated desert destination. I find myself wondering what my grandfather, the Afghan writer Ikbal Ali Shah, would have thought of the city now. He first visited there back in the 1930s, shortly before Winston Churchill brought Franklin D. Roosevelt to stay at La Mamounia during the War, to soak up the light. On the face of it, the change has been extraordinary – a surge of people, cars and buildings.

But look in a different way.

Close your eyes and let the city touch your other senses, and you begin to appreciate that Marrakech is today what it has always been – a crucible of all that is exotic.

From: *Marrakech: The Red City*

# Morocco

OVER THE PAST fifteen years I've published a lot of material on Morocco – two travel books, a novel, and dozens of magazine articles, as well as introductions to books by others, radio broadcasts, videos, and all kinds of other work.

The more I've churned out about Morocco, and the more I've thought about that rare and magical land, the more I have realized that I know the country in a limited way.

The day you wake up and scream: 'Oh my God! I don't know the place I'm supposed to be an expert on!' is a cherished moment. Reach that point and, like an apprentice carpenter, you can cross a threshold to a new realm.

*The Magic Zone.*

All of a sudden it's as though you see clues that were hidden to you before. You find that you can take what you know and rotate it in your mind – as if you're no longer restricted. For the first time, you see things in Cinemascope.

When I bought Dar Khalifa, a rambling old mansion in the middle of a Casablanca shantytown, I held on tight and prepared myself for a rollercoaster ride. That ride certainly came, jerking us left and right, up, down, and over and over in loops. Nothing that ever took place was what I expected.

For me, that's the magic of Morocco.

In Europe I'm sometimes found moaning that it's all so safe and predictable. You add 1 to 1 and you get 2. But, in Morocco, the same sum will give you a total of 5, or 2732, or 2.998, or sometimes even 2.

Rather like a one-armed bandit at an amusement arcade, you never quite know what the next sequence will be. On occasions you do of course come up with nothing – but more often than not, the result is an unexpected treasure trail of wonder.

As with travels anywhere in the Magic Zone, you have to be prepared to receive what's on offer. Most travellers are never tuned properly to pick up the full bandwidth. For that reason, they aren't given the entry pass into the Magic Zone. You have to earn it by grasping what your senses show you, and by flipping it inside out and back to front.

Retune your channels of perception, look at what's being shot your way, and Morocco opens up. As with any place that I've come to know well, the joy is in the kind of thing only a local would ever notice.

If I could encapsulate Morocco in one such detail it would be this:

Stroll down any backstreet in Casablanca, or any other city in the kingdom, slow your pace, and look around.

Within a minute or two you're likely to notice a scrap of bread up on a wall, or on a window ledge. A visitor probably wouldn't see it. A Moroccan would see it and know why it was there.

The reason is this: the Prophet said that a beggar has as much honour as a rich man, and that as such he should not have to stoop to pick up a crust of stray bread.

For this reason, little crusts are picked up with care, dusted off, and put where they might be received by those in need.

Such details, that appear too insignificant to be noticed, are the essence of Morocco.

From: *Morocco: The Anthologies*

# Paris Syndrome

THIS NOVEL WAS sparked into life by a short article featured on the BBC website.

Describing how, each year, numerous Japanese tourists visiting the French capital were overcome by a mysterious ailment, it ended with the most magical and infectious line:

'The only permanent cure is to go back to Japan – never to return to Paris.'

As so often happens to me, that single sentence embedded itself in my mind, drilling away at my attention – in daydreams and in sleep.

During my early twenties, I'd spent almost a year and a half living in Japan, and was a great admirer of all things Japanese. Like all the other *gaijin*, I'd been lured by the thought of making fast cash teaching English. But, unlike them, the moment I arrived in Tokyo, I grasped that being an English teacher would be to cast away what was a mesmerizing opportunity… an opportunity to root through the intertwined layers of Japanese life.

I have described the highs and lows of my life in Japan elsewhere, so won't revisit them again in detail here. Needless to say, finding myself in what was then the most expensive city on earth, and without any income at all, I was broker than broke.

Having been moved on from a variety of sordid lodgings, each one twice as abhorrent as the last, I was taken in by fellow writer-to-be, Robert Twigger. I spent my days learning about the indigenous Ainu people of the Japanese archipelago, and my nights sleeping beneath the dining table.

Twigger and I got into a routine of playing chess competitively, speaking about all the books we would one day write, while listening to a single song on a looped cassette. Close my eyes and I hear it even now – Lucienne Boyer's 1930 hit 'Parlez-moi d'amour'.

One evening, as we sat there, moving homemade chess pieces around a homemade board, Twigger looked over at me, his expression quizzical.

'D'you think we'll ever write books?'

'Of course we will!'

'How can you be so sure?'

'Well, look at us… we're no good for anything else.'

Twigger winced, uncertain whether to take offence. As he did so, I made a solemn promise to myself, to write books on a grand scale, and to use all the material that ever presented itself to me.


Eventually I left Japan, and returned to Britain by way of Africa, where I stayed in Samburuland with my friend, the explorer Wilfred Thesiger.

I travelled to a great many places, most of them far beyond the reaches of Europe. As anyone who's read my travel books will know, I sought out oddity and eccentricity, until the adventures rubbed off on me, making me the eccentric oddball I'd been searching for.

Even though I was obsessed with far-flung climes, I visited all the other places as well, the kind conventional people frequent – places like Paris. I never wrote about them because they seemed far too sedate. Through the lens with which I viewed the world, they may have been serene, but they were dull.

In the case of Paris, that all changed on the morning I read the BBC piece about Paris Syndrome. It was as though the French capital was luring me close, offering an olive branch – an olive branch of oddity.

Grasping it with both hands, I slipped back into the impecunious mindset I'd had while living in Japan. I recollected all the industrious office staff, the attention to detail, and the preoccupation with all things Parisian.

Before I knew it, *Paris Syndrome* had written itself in my mind.

I could see Miki and her journey in glorious Technicolor.

Most of all, though, I could see a way of telling what I knew about Japan through the lens of another place.

Any other writer with a deep fascination for Japan would, and throughout history has, written about the country directly. The way I perceived it, my interest with Japan was with the culture rather than the physical destination.

Considering the culture while *in situ* was rather too obvious. Far more interesting, as far as I was concerned, was reflecting upon it when held at a distance from itself.

In describing Miki's trials and tribulations, I allowed myself to descend down through layers of bewitching misery until I'd reached a bedrock – the bedrock of mania. I've employed the theme in other books, such as in my search for the lost Incan city of Paititi, *House of the Tiger King*, and in my novel, *Eye Spy*, about a surgeon who goes off the rails in the most spectacular way.

When *Paris Syndrome* was launched, I received dozens of emails – some from people who'd adored the book, and others from people who had an axe to grind over the treatment of my fictional protagonist – as one reader described her – 'poor indefensible Miki'.

One message was unlike all the rest.

Sent by a Japanese woman named Manami, and written in good English, it explained how she had succumbed to so-called 'Paris Syndrome' six years before, while visiting the French capital for the first time.

'You may think I am crazy,' she wrote, 'but I am not. I am a normal woman. When I see crazy things, I cross the street and hurry away.'

Manami and I corresponded by email a couple of times, as she did her best to explain from the inside out what it had been like to suffer from Paris Syndrome. Time passed, and I almost forgot about her.

Then, one afternoon, I saw a message from her in my email inbox.

'I am coming to London,' she wrote. 'We can meet and have tea.'

A week later, I found myself sitting in the window of a bustling, old-fashioned café on Piccadilly. I'd arrived early, and was sipping a cup of Lapsang Souchong.

Waiters were hurrying back and forth, platters of pastries on their arms.

As I took a journal from my canvas bag, something caught

my attention – the lace hem of a dress, sweeping through the door.

I looked up.

A frail young woman with a complexion like antique porcelain stepped forward. Dressed impeccably in lace, her dainty hand held a matching parasol.

She smiled, bowed, and smiled a second time.

I stood up, smiled, bowed, smiled again, and invited Manami to sit.

For more than an hour we spoke about travels in the usual places, about people we had encountered, and things we'd both seen. The conversation was more delightful to me than any I could remember.

Thinking about it now, I believe the reason was that, through Manami, I was reliving my own adventures in Japan.

Ninety minutes into our rendezvous, we both fell silent. Sitting there, we stared at our laps, as though drained of words.

'Will you tell me about your experience in Paris?' I asked gently.

Manami's lips parted, her head tilted, and she sucked in air through the sides of her mouth – a Japanese indication of awkwardness.

'It was a difficult time,' she said with understatement.

'I quite understand if you'd rather not talk about it.'

Sucking in more air, Manami held up a hand, then grinned anxiously.

'I will tell you,' she said.

Another pot of Lapsang Souchong was served.

Manami opened an expensive-looking leather handbag and took out a lace handkerchief, which matched the parasol and dress.

'I will need this,' she said. 'You see, talking about my experience always makes me weep.'

'You weep from the pain of memory?'

'No, no,' Manami said. 'I do not weep from pain. I weep from shame at how silly I was.'

For more than an hour she described the intricate details of her brush with Paris Syndrome, helping me to understand the condition from the inside out.

She described the causes of the mania, the hot flushes, the ranting, the delirium, and the cure. In her case, the treatment involved being taken to a small psychiatric unit in Brittany.

From time to time, Manami wept, just as she'd said she would. Dabbing her eyes with the lace, she apologized.

'I am a silly woman,' she said. 'A silly woman who brought shame to her family and friends.'

'Of course you're not,' I replied sincerely. 'We have all found ourselves overwhelmed at some time.'

Manami dabbed her eye, slipped the lace square back in her handbag, and said:

'When I read *Paris Syndrome* I wondered how you would be.'

'And how am I?' I asked with a grin.

'You are a kind man,' said Manami.

'Why do you say that?'

'Because you are polite, and politeness is important.'

I agreed that it was.

'And...' Manami uttered in no more than a whisper.

'*And...?*'

'And you are kind because you gave your novel a happy ending.'

From: *Paris Syndrome*

# *People*

FROM EARLY CHILDHOOD my sisters and I were encouraged to start collections.

Looking back, it was a pursuit inspired by my parents' own youth. Trawl through eBay and you'll find thousands of albums containing everything from postage stamps to bookmarks, and from beer mats to luggage labels. Assembled over the precious years of childhood, the yellowed pages are a testament to youthful diligence.

One Christmas, we were given albums by our eccentric and favourite aunt, Amina.

'I'm going to collect pictures of butterflies,' said Safia.

'I'm going to collect foreign banknotes,' said Saira.

'I'm going to collect people,' I said.

And that's just what I did.

While my sisters worked away at their more practical collections, I filled my album with material of a quite different nature. Although hindered by truly terrible handwriting, I collected descriptions of people I knew.

At first, the people I detailed were Mrs. Ellard, the housekeeper, our beloved nanny Pauline, George the handyman, and my father's secretary, Helena. Then, I branched out to take in the village's regular cast – Mrs. Knock at the post office, where we bought sweets with our pocket money; Mr. Lovett the butcher; and the prim lady with no lips behind the counter at the bakery.

After a few weeks I got into my stride. Whenever anyone stepped in through the front door, I would observe them from my position at the top of the stairs. Like an eagle perched on a high vantage point I watched intently, noting down details that seemed important to me – such as how they smelled, what they were dressed in, and whether they moved slow or fast. Sometimes I would try to find out who the visitors were. More often than not I was shooed away and told to go up to the playroom. In such cases I gave them a codename instead.

A sample entry read:

*Poncho-man: Beard. Long hair. Happy. Blue poncho. First time I have seen him. Smells of expensive cheese. Maybe from Mexico. Seemed in a hurry to talk to Baba. Study door closed when he arrived. Tea served by Mrs. Ellard. Laughed when door to study opened. Waved to me sitting on the stairs. Shouted 'Hola!' Hope he comes back.*

As the years passed, my people collection went from strength to strength, as I made note of almost everyone who came down on the weekends. Most of the visitors were not well known, and many of those who were had been given invented names.

One afternoon I sat on the floor of the small sitting-room with my people collection. Behind me, my mother was knitting, her lips counting stitches.

'One day you'll be able to sell that for a lot, darling,' she said.

I gasped at the comment.

'Couldn't sell it!' I exclaimed, clutching the album to my chest.

'You've got some famous people in there.'

'But they're not for sale.'

'Not even for a million pounds?'

'No! Not even for a billion pounds!'

My mother looked down at me, her hands knitting on autopilot.

'I am pleased to hear it,' she said. 'Because some things should never be bought or sold.'

The next week I took the album to my prep school with the intention of expanding some of the entries during break. I'd never planned to write notes on any of the teachers. They were such a rotten bunch I didn't want them in my beloved collection. But a sudden urge to collect caused me to break my own rule.

At the end of prep we were dismissed with some nonsensical phrase in Latin, by an ex-army-monocle-tweed-clad master. As I took the album out from my desk, he beckoned me forward.

'What's that, young man?' he snarled accusingly.

'Nothing, sir.'

'Nothing? How can it be nothing? It's not nothing… it's something!'

'It's an album, sir.'

'Stamps?'

'No, sir.'

'If not stamps, then what?!'

'People, sir.'

'People?!'

'Yes, sir.'

'How can it be people?! Show it to me!'

Gingerly, I passed over the people collection. Slotting his

monocle into place, the retired major regarded the pages fast, grunting with disdain – while I prayed.

My prayers were not answered.

Cheeks flushing beetroot in rage, his mouth snarled, his monocle popped out and dangled on its chain.

'How dare you?!' he roared.

'Very sorry, sir.'

Thrusting left and right, he smashed the side of my head with the book.

'Going to burn it! Going to burn this wretched filth!'

Turning on his heel, the retired major stormed away, my people collection under his arm. It was a great sadness, and one I've never quite recovered from – not least because the final entry, a list, was incomplete:

*Major Smith:*

*Grey hair*

*Pocket watch*

*Red and black zigzag tie*

*Calls lunch 'luncheon', and forces us to eat it with sliced white bread*

*Teaches maths*

*Cruel*

*Loud*

*Rude*

*Enjoys beating boys for no reason at all*

*Hope he goes to Hell…*

From: *People: The Anthologies*

# Quest

THE FIRST TIME I ever heard the word 'quest' was in a Nasrudin story:

The wise fool Nasrudin had caught word that there was a cave filled with a magnificent treasure hidden in the jungles of Sumatra. Dropping everything, he put together an expedition, and hacked through the seething forests on a monumental quest.

A year to the day on which he had set out, his team reached the mouth of the cave – having done so through a series of coincidences and unlikely good fortune. Ordering the porters to hold back, Nasrudin lit a burning torch and strode inside, his imagination stoked with visions of golden treasure.

Although spacious, the cave was empty.

In place of riches was a wooden box, inscribed with cryptic symbols. Rushing over, the wise fool opened it and found a message, which read:

'Congratulations on reaching the most valuable treasure in the world! Rather than being in an obvious form, it is presented in the shape of this message and this box. Together they contain pointers which will be easily understood by anyone wise enough to have followed the clues to this cave.'

Stamping his feet, Nasrudin cursed his bad luck.

'What provision do you provide for those guided not by wisdom, but by serendipity?!' he cried.

Over the decades that I've travelled and written books, I

have found there's nothing to get the juices of enthusiasm or creativity flowing like a monumental quest.

Whether searching for the fabled gold mines of King Solomon, or the secret to the riddle of primitive flight, the 'quest' theme sets the stage for potential glory, and keeps the humble adventurer on track. Or, rather, it allows him to go off track, once the path has been scoped out.

In the back-to-front world in which I tend to reside, there's only one thing as important as having a quest: not reaching the desired goal – or at least not via an obvious route. The way I perceive such things, a journey is as much about changing oneself as it is about reaching the destination.

Aim high and off-piste, and you're promised an extravaganza like none other – allowing a quest to take shape by shunting it into a twilight zone of implausible possibility.

Ask any writer who has published more than a usual amount, and they'll tell you how they receive a mass of mail – in whatever form it reaches them. Unlike many authors, I believe that hearing from readers is important – and I do my utmost to reply to everyone who messages me. Although I write for myself alone, feedback from readers is helpful to me.

Every week I receive many dozens of messages from people who want to follow quests as I have done. They come in thick and fast through social media and emails, via the publishers who represent me, by mail, and occasionally by visitors who turn up at my door. About two-thirds of them are young people who are desperate to embark on a great quest. Enthusiastic and inexperienced, they don't usually know how to get started.

One of my few strengths is that I never let circumstances get in the way. While being completely broke I've planned and raised funds for massive expeditions. Impecuniosity is the most perfect motivator for thinking big.

When receiving such pleas for advice, I almost always reply in the same way – with a list:

1. Get a sheet of A4 paper and a pen.
2. Sit in a comfortable chair and close your eyes.
3. Think of five incredible things that interest you.
4. Turn them around in your mind as you observe their wonder.
5. Open your eyes and list the things, however odd.
6. Try to link them to an ultimate goal – even if it's unattainable.
7. Think zigzag and not straight, because a straight route never got anyone anywhere worth going.
8. Don't talk about your idea, but live with it – developing it a little at a time.
9. Don't stress about raising funds. If you've allowed the idea to grow sufficiently in your imagination, it will take shape and become real.
10. Most of all, don't ever listen to anyone who tells you that you're incapable. Naysayers are passengers in human society – the people the leaders drag behind them as they move ahead in search of their quest.

From: *Quest: The Anthologies*

## Scorpion Soup

SINCE EARLY CHILDHOOD, I was raised with the notion of a Chain of Transmission.

It's the idea that progress is made by layers of action, achievement, and thought – layers laid down through a group, or even by members of a single family. In my case, the latter was very much the focus of attention.

My father, the writer and thinker Idries Shah, devoted his life to making certain psychological and philosophical traditions available to the West. Much of the material he presented had of course been in existence there for centuries. But, more often than not, it was as though the thinking was a valuable tool, kept in a glass case – viewed with awe, but rarely actually used.

Like a relay runner in a race, my father was the one who passed me the baton, urging me to run with it, until it was my time to pass it on. He, in turn, had been entrusted it by his father, The Sirdar Ikbal Ali Shah, who'd been handed it by his own father.

This theme of a Chain of Transmission runs through my family's core, and is regarded as more important than anything else. Of greater consequence than any single member of the family, it constitutes a kind of mass Group Think... a Group Think that embraces me, my father, and grandfather, my great grandfather, and all those who came before them. It's my mother and grandmother, too, my aunts, uncles, cousins, and all the rest – forming a single unified contribution to human society, bridging East with West.

My father used to explain how, whether I understood it or not, I was part of a machinery that was laden with certain responsibilities. He went on and on about it, sometimes filling me with dread and fear – as it would have any small child. I didn't understand why I couldn't be like all the other kids in the school playground, why I had to be part of a Chain of Transmission that seemed to make no sense at all.

As the years passed, and as I began to understand the world and its ingrained systems, I learned that change takes time. Beyond that, I learned that it takes a group effort, as well as recalibration through increments.

One of the most fundamental aspects of the Chain of Transmission I was handed, and expected to pass on, relates to what you might call 'Looped Thinking'. It's the sense that by circling back over the same ground in different ways, we learn to absorb ideas. And, once we've learned to absorb, we're ready to apply what we've learned.

The reason I'm explaining all this is not to try and impress anyone reading it with what I, or members of my family, have ever been exposed to. Rather, I am hoping to pass on something else – something related to Looped Thinking and the Chain of Transmission...

You could call it 'Framing'.

As those who've read any of *The Thousand and One Nights* knows, the story is set up in a curious way. Having discovered that his queen has been unfaithful, King Shahriyar resorts to marrying a virgin bride each day, and having her executed at dawn.

This barbaric practice continues, until that is, the

daughter of the Grand Vizier, whose name is Scheherazade, marries the king and begins to tell him a story... a story that at dawn remains unfinished. Intrigued how it ends, he allows his new bride to keep her throat for another day.

Each evening, the story continues... for a thousand and one nights. In that time, certain ideas, themes, and bodies of information are revisited time and again. And, as the story moves forward, certain tales spring off into other tales which, in turn, give forth to framed stories of their own.

At one point there are nine tales in play.

Imagine it...

A tale, in a tale, in a tale, in a tale, in a tale, in a tale, in a tale, in a tale, in a tale.

This framing appears as a tool in other Oriental treasuries, and has been copied throughout history. Chaucer borrowed the device for his *Canterbury Tales*. And, more recently, in the 1930s, my grandfather employed it in his *The Golden Pilgrimage*. In that volume, a group of travellers thrown together at a remote caravanserai share stories, in stories.

After reading *The Golden Pilgrimage* as a child, I longed to create a looped structure that would eventually circle back to its beginning, while encompassing the kind of themes and ideas I'd been raised to pass on.

I never planned for *Scorpion Soup* to be that book.

Indeed, I never planned it at all.

One drab Monday morning, having slouched down into my office chair at Dar Khalifa, my Moroccan home, I read a grim message from an equally grim publisher, ordering me to knock out a book I didn't want to knock out.

I remember reading the threatening email three or four times, and sighing long and hard. The last thing any writer wants to do is to create where there's no creative spark.

So, having sighed three or four more times, I let my attention drift from the computer screen, over the desk, and out through the open doors of my library… into the garden.

I saw myself wandering down to Casablanca's port.

The next thing I knew, I'd begun…

…begun the tale that was to spiral down, down, down, through a series of tales, before the last line looped back to the first.

In most cases I love the writing process more than I can describe. I love the business of transforming a blank screen, or a blank page, into a document that changes the way people see the world around them. I love the raw ingenuity of the writer's craft. And I love the way a book can be a kind of Trojan horse, a container for ideas, themes, and values, all of them far more important than the characters, or the storyline.

I think it would be true to say that I loved writing *Scorpion Soup* more than any other book I've ever written – because it was a book that truly wrote itself.

As I typed, I would watch my hands from a distance, as though they weren't mine… in the same way that a puppeteer must marvel at their hands having taken on a lifeblood all of their own.

The way I see it, *Scorpion Soup* was a story that my fantastical alter ego gave the rest of me as a gift, a daydream…

…a reminder that since childhood I was charged with

passing on the baton, itself a loop of collected culture – my small part in the Chain of Transmission.

From: *Scorpion Soup*

## Seven League Boots

GOOD TRAVEL WRITING is as much about the author as it is the destination.

Through twists and turns on the map, you glimpse both strengths and weaknesses of character, and learn to love or loathe your hero as they drag you on towards an ultimate goal.

As an aficionado of travel literature, I am drawn to those who lead from the front, the hard-as-nails breed who keep on going – even in the face of disastrous odds. Nothing gives me more pleasure than to witness an author enduring the unendurable without the faintest whimper of distress. This form of true-grit travel writing is, of course, the preserve of the Victorian greats – Richard Burton, Samuel White Baker and Heinrich Barth among them. Adventurers first and writers second, their books are charged with an underlying emotion, one forged through sheer determination.

For readers who already know his work, it may seem odd to link Richard Halliburton to the Victorian legends. Not naturally tough, he tackled every expedition with such a wall of raw enthusiasm that his detractors couldn't help but respect him.

My own fascination for Halliburton stems from the fact he always set the bar ridiculously high. Embarking on near-impossible quests with almost no preparation, he careened onward, propelled by natural charisma and by a lust for adventure matched by no man.

On turbulent, storm-ridden nights in the Amazon

rainforest, or at sea, I have clung to the memory of Halliburton, a hero who took adversity squarely on the chin. However excruciating my own journeys have been, it's comforting to know that Halliburton suffered as much or more, and without ever making a point of it.

Born into a comfortably middle-class Tennessee family in January 1900, his ill-health through childhood confined him to bed for long stretches of time. Eventually he wound up at the legendary Battle Creek Sanitarium, presided over by the indefatigable John Harvey Kellogg (of the cornflakes fame). Perusing his life, you get the feeling that Halliburton had a plan mapped out right from the start. He recognized the key steps that would springboard him into the world of celebrity – the first of which was attending Princeton, and the second of which was acquiring well-placed friends.

Throughout his short life he used his friendships for inspiration, as he did his obsession for those towering figures of adventure he knew only by reputation. The mountaineer George Mallory was a man who influenced him greatly, all the more when he perished on his 1924 attempt to conquer Everest. Rudolf Valentino impressed him for sheer on-screen bravado, and showed that the fledgling technology of cinema was the way forward.

And it was technology that shaped Halliburton's work. At a time when cars and aeroplanes were unreliable at best, he set out on mechanized quests, capturing all he could on moving celluloid. I can think of no other early twentieth-century traveller who so quickly grasped the need to make the weekly newsreels, or a splash on the front pages, as a way of getting hype for his daredevil feats of adventure.

His sixth book, *Seven League Boots* appeared in 1935, and is a rollercoaster ride of travel through fragments of America, Russia, Ethiopia, Arabia and the Alps. As with most of his other books, Halliburton didn't give much time to planning the journey, but allowed it to percolate forth on whim, obsession, and abounding curiosity.

The highlights are the face-to-face meetings with men and women who had shaped history, people whom Richard Halliburton managed to get close to. He interviewed, for example, one of Czar Nicholas's assassins, as well as Lenin's widow, King Ibn Saud, and Emperor Haile Selassie of Ethiopia. The great quality of this book is the irresistible charm – Halliburton's charm – effortless and unending. Using it like a magic wand, he cornered some of the biggest names of the time, presenting his readers with a snapshot of a world they themselves would never see.

One evening in Addis Ababa he found himself at a private dinner with Haile Selassie. At a time when Abyssinia was at war with the Italians, the Emperor was making the most of Halliburton's journalistic contacts. The American, it seems, wasn't the only one at the table with an understanding of mass media.

If the interviews with people are the mortar, then the bricks are Halliburton's forthright descriptions of the places themselves. As a journalist writing copy he learned the art of telling it like it was, a skill unknown to many of his contemporaries. I love the way he got under the skin of a place, commenting on a people and their system at a key point in history. He wrote of Russia, for example:

> When I sat down in Moscow to write my story, I found it strangely unmanageable. To write forcefully and well about this infuriating but astounding country, one must have definite convictions and opinions. But in keeping with the experience of most other foreigners, my convictions suffered such violent and such frequent changes that I hardly knew myself from day to day what I believed.
>
> Each morning, having to face the bayonet-regimented existence in Moscow, I swore anew that the rule of the Soviets was the most cruel, most brutal, and most colossal racket ever rammed at pistol point down the throats of a helpless people. And yet before night I would have seen some isolated feature of Bolshevism that was so enlightened, so advanced and so inspiring, that for the moment I forgot the tyranny that had produced it.

Yet for all the detail of people and place, a travel book with Richard Halliburton's name embossed on the cover couldn't exist without a good solid chunk of awe-inspiring bravado. The same Halliburton who had followed in Byron's footsteps swimming the Hellespont, or circumnavigated the globe on an aeroplane of little more than canvas and glue, had to wow his readers with a feat that made history... again.

Taking the lead from none other than Hannibal, the

indefatigable American got himself a timid French circus elephant – called Elysabethe Dalrymple – and set about crossing the Alps at the St. Bernard Pass. The result was Halliburton at his finest, playing to the cameras and adoring the publicity, another achievement for the history books.

His life abounding in highs and lows, as America's favourite explorer of the pre-War years, Richard Halliburton had precious little time left. Within four years he disappeared along with his crew, and their craft – a Chinese junk named *Sea Dragon*. No one knows exactly where they went down, except that they were three weeks out from Hong Kong, in the wide waters of the Pacific.

Richard Halliburton may have perished, but his memory, and his marvellous books, live on.

From: *Seven League Boots*

# Sorcerer's Apprentice

I NEVER PLANNED to write *Sorcerer's Apprentice*.

Setting down my experiences amid the underbelly of Indian magic was the furthest thing from my mind. The haphazard journeys I had made through the subcontinent on the heels of illusion were very personal adventures – adventures I never expected to share with anyone.

They were part of my preoccupation with the kind of stage magic that was pioneered by Harry Houdini, and by others, more than a century ago.

From the first moment I reached India, I was transfixed by the intense cultural colour. It hit me like a bucket of iced water, and was like nothing I had ever experienced before. Whereas Europe is so often little more than thin consommé, India is a mesmerizing, intoxicating goulash of a land.

I found that I couldn't help but drink it all in – feasting on the details and the interwoven layers of life. For the first time ever I felt that I had arrived at a place with a full spectrum. There was more life in a few feet of the Kolkata pavement than in entire cities elsewhere. And, as I was to learn, the most ordinary-looking people were the gatekeepers into a world of mystery and marvel, the kind of place that has bewitched Occidental travellers for centuries.

When I wrote *Sorcerer's Apprentice*, the critics were kind but rather disbelieving. Some of them even implied that I'd made the whole thing up. What I have been trying to explain ever since the first copies hit bookshop shelves is that this is a story of India – a land where the unbelievable is the norm.

I wish people who don't get this point would leave their tedious lives in Europe, North America or wherever, and would travel to the Indian subcontinent. If they left right away, they could be having breakfast there tomorrow morning... and they'd understand that India is a realm crafted in a magic of its own.

As for myself, I was well aware that the idea of writing of my experiences with the incomparable magician, Hakim Feroze, would be extremely unpopular with him.

And they were.

Feroze telephoned me one Monsoon night. I could hear the rain coming down in sheets behind him. And I can remember the quavering anger in his voice. As soon as I had heard the *click click* of the international line, I'd known it was Feroze. He was fuming. As far as he was concerned, I had denigrated my time with him to fodder for a travel book.

It is a view that upset me greatly.

I have always held Feroze in the highest respect. When he died in 2001, I felt an emptiness that I have rarely experienced. It was a sense that a life had ended that could never be lived again.

Hindsight is the most remarkable privilege.

I can now look back with some amusement at the trials and tribulations to which I was subjected, a sadistic pleasure for the Master. And I can smile at it all.

But, far more importantly, I can see that what Feroze had wanted was for me to be exposed to levels of thought and understanding that pass almost everyone else by. He reduced me to my raw mettle and, only then, began the laborious process of building me up.

The quest for illusion was what had kept my attention, and was the catalyst that had got me started. But it wasn't the thing of real value. The value was in learning to see what I thought I understood with fresh eyes.

My favourite axiom is from Arabia – *Much travel is needed before the raw man is ripened.* There is no place better for ripening rawness than India. And there's no better way at opening oneself to being ripened than following a quest. It's a theme which has run through much of my work, because I have learned that a quest – however inane and zigzag – can open doors that had been invisible before.

I spend my life encouraging young people to head off into the wild unknown without preparing, or giving a journey too much thought. We live in a society that's obsessed with preparation, with planning, and with analyzing, but one that is blinkered to the Oriental concept of absorbing through cultural osmosis.

Stand on a street corner in any Indian city, with the maelstrom of traffic swirling around you.

Close your eyes.

Take a deep breath, and let it all wash in.

You can be certain of one thing: that you will leave a very different person than when you arrived.

From: *Sorcerer's Apprentice*

## South

THE FIRST TIME I crossed the equator into the southern hemisphere was on a KLM flight from Amsterdam to Nairobi, in the first week of January 1986.

Nineteen years old, I was venturing to sub-Saharan Africa to study at a small American university there. Shortly after breakfast, a turquoise-clad flight attendant came to where I was scrunched up in economy.

'First time?' she asked brightly.

'First time for what?'

'Flying south of the equator.'

I nodded.

'Yes.'

The attendant handed me a certificate.

'Fill out the name yourself.'

Since then I've crossed the equator on dozens of occasions – in the air, on the ocean, and on land as well. Most of the time I don't think about it, because it doesn't really matter. After all, the invisible line marked red on globes and world maps only holds the significance we place upon it.

Economists like to drone on about the North-South divide, as do geographers, and all kinds of academic types. On reading their theories, as I tend to do, I find myself groaning at their deductions. I'm not interested in comparing North and South, just as it doesn't interest me to contrast East with West.

What does interest me is observing the southern hemisphere of our planet, without contrasting it to the north. I'm drawn to the study of considering the southern hemisphere by itself. And, better still, by the pursuit of searching out its individual wonders.

In the early nineties, I travelled to the Seychelles and spent several weeks roaming that Indian Ocean archipelago. Although pretending I was on the trail of certain spices, I was in actual fact searching for buried pirate treasure.

In 1721, Olivier Levasseur, known as La Buse – 'The Buzzard' – plundered a Portuguese ship called *Virgem do Cabo*. Fearing for his life, he supposedly hid the treasure – valued at more than a billion dollars – on the island of Mahé. The hoard is said to have contained a vast amount of gold coins, as well as the seven-foot tall Cross of Goa, encrusted with precious gems, and fashioned from the purest gold.

An encoded treasure cryptogram was in circulation at the time. A great many adventurers had spent months, and even years, interpreting it. Shunning their deductions, I used my knowledge of the Abjad – an ancient Arabic system of transcription and divination – to make sense of the map.

While my budget held out, I searched for the treasure and had all kinds of adventures on Mahé, and on a number of the other islands.

One evening I sought sanctuary in a bar on the beach, reflecting how I was the only single foreigner in the entire country. Couples, and especially honeymoon couples, frequented the islands. As a result, almost every dish on every restaurant menu was prepared for two, from Chateaubriand steak to Crêpes Suzette.

While sitting at the bar, watching the sun slip graciously

into the Indian Ocean, I was approached by a boisterous Seychellois. Reeling theatrically from side to side, he was clutching a half-empty bottle of rotgut palm rum.

'Looking for the treasure, aren't you?!' he yelled, his slurred words spoken in French.

'News travels fast,' I said.

'There are no secrets on Mahé, my friend.'

'So do you have any tips for a treasure hunter?'

Taking a good, long swig from the bottle, the man punched a fist up into the air.

'We look for treasure because it excites our dreams,' he cried. 'There's no hope of finding it, but it doesn't matter at all. What matters is being changed by the experience of adventure!'

A moment or two later, the drunk man and his lengthening shadow had vanished. But what he said to me in that fleeting encounter stuck with me in the most profound way.

In the years that followed, I searched for magic, lost cities, prehistoric cave systems, hidden manuscripts, and yet more treasure. Each time I chose a quest, I made sure it was even more captivating than the one before. Of course I knew the odds were stacked against me. But like the drunk on the beach had grasped so keenly, there's no need to actually find the treasure.

The important thing is to embrace adventure and find oneself.

From: *South: The Anthologies*

# Taboo

As I UNDERSTAND it, Captain Cook brought the word 'taboo' back with him on his journey from Polynesia, in which *tabu* was used in the Tongan dialect to mean 'forbidden'.

Certain ideas and values fascinate me profoundly.

One of them is the way society permits all kinds of things and prohibits others – often for no apparent reason. I'm not saying all taboo behaviour is right. A good many carnal practices are most definitely wrong, as are other offensive ways of conduct. But it seems to me as though individual societies are programmed to condone certain acts and to shun others.

I've been extraordinarily privileged to experience layers of life that most people never have the chance to observe. My good fortune lies in my restless nature, coupled with a burning desire to drill down through layers. Never satisfied with witnessing a place in an obvious one-dimensional way, I prefer to challenge myself when observing anything – from a mug of hot tea at a street-side stall in Tibet, to the perilous stretch of Interstate 10 between Phoenix and California.

The draw for me is to dissect what I'm presented with through the various lenses in my armoury. My favourite is the lens of absurdity – the kind meted out by the wise fool, Nasrudin. Another is the lens of making connections: linking one stray detail to another, until patterns emerge. A third is a lens devoted to identifying layers that are buried so deep that they've never been seen – not even by the locals.

As I zigzag around the world, I'm drawn to anything that's perceived to be off-limits – whether it be a way of behaving, thinking, or operating. At the same time, I am attracted in a magnetic way to societies that exhibit a counter-culture set against that of the Occidental one in which I was raised.

In my early twenties, I went in search of the communities in Madagascar in which twins are regarded as cursed – so much so that they are often abandoned at birth. Being a twin myself, I was intrigued at how such a profound part of me was regarded as utterly taboo.

Village elders explained their reasoning by saying that twins were rejected because they brought misfortune on the community. The mothers of twins I met told me that they were at fault, and had begged forgiveness for producing unacceptable offspring.

Before leaving Madagascar, I visited one last village in which far more twins than normal were living. Like me, most of them were fraternal and not identical. I assumed women who had given birth to twins had taken refuge there, but was informed this was not the case. Rather, the numbers were due to an above-average incidence of twins being born.

I enquired whether the standard taboo was maintained in the village. The mothers to whom I was speaking all broke into laughter and wagged their hands left and right.

'Of course not!' one exclaimed. 'Look at us – does it look as though we're cursed?!'

'We're blessed twice over!' a second woman cried out.

Not long after I departed Madagascar, I read about an anthropologist in a French newspaper who'd been working

191

to rid the island of the taboo. Having raised funding through an NGO, he gave large donations to villages in which twins were born. The money was reserved for communal projects rather than for the families of twins.

Within a few months, the newspaper article explained, the reluctant elders dropped the taboo, and pocketed the cash. Delighted at the news, I saw it as a victory for sanity.

Years later, I read another piece about the same Madagascan village. I expected to learn how the taboo was long since gone. But it was not the case. When the anthropologist and his funding had disappeared a decade earlier, the prohibition on twins had returned.

Foreign support for villages with twins dried up, and life became very hard indeed in communities that had relied on the money. People who had learned to live with small luxuries found themselves destitute once again – unprepared for poverty.

Enraged, the village elders asserted that the foreign money, and the withdrawal of it, had been yet another manifestation of the curse of twins.

From: *Taboo: The Anthologies*

# The Caliph's House

THE WAY I see it, Dar Khalifa isn't so much of a house, as a love affair, a teller of tales, and a crucible of dreams.

I've tried to describe the way that bewitching structure slipped into my life, and how it shaped our lives. The preceding pages present my perceptions of the first year. The story is first and foremost about my connection to Dar Khalifa, and mine alone.

When *The Caliph's House* appeared, I had no idea it would become the sensation it ultimately did. I hoped it would bring a smile to the faces of readers, but had no way of perceiving the mass of attention it garnered.

A week after the book was released to the trade in the United States, I received a message from a librarian. As I remember, she was in a small city somewhere in the great heartland of Nebraska.

'Your book transported me to Morocco,' she wrote. 'But that's not why I liked it so much. A great many books are place-transporters, or time-machines. What counts is what they do to you once they've whisked you away to far off climes. Your memoir of Morocco sung to me, not in an obvious way, but in one that tethered me to the land you described.'

In writing *The Caliph's House*, I was focused on a single mission – to show Morocco to those who didn't know it, or at least to those who didn't know it in the way I myself had experienced it.

Published four years after 9/11, I hoped the book would

play a small part in recalibrating the communal Occidental appreciation for Morocco. I am no expert on all things Moroccan but, as an admirer of the kingdom, I feel a deep-down duty to show what the Land of Sunset is, and what it is not.

It is a magical realm of ancient culture, etiquette, traditions and, perhaps beyond all else, of stories. At the same time, it's not a land of fanaticism, or a hotbed of unrest.

Morocco is itself.

I adore that about it, more than anything else – that it's not trying to be anything it isn't.

In the years that have passed since *The Caliph's House* was released, I've watched with delight as others have been affected by the same dazzling joy that first touched me as a toddler, sitting in my grandfather's garden in Tangier.

Translated into at least thirty languages, the book has found itself in the hands of people who may never have an opportunity to visit the kingdom, or at least to know it as I've had the privilege to do.

In my book *The Reason to Write*, I described how there's a constant flow of visitors arriving at Dar Khalifa's doors. Some spend their life savings to make the journey, while others drop by because they happened to be on the other side of town.

Since describing our first year at Dar Khalifa, a tumultuous wind of change has blown through. The *bidonville* has gone, replaced by apartment buildings rising three storeys into the North African sky. Our friends in the shantytown have been moved on – in most cases to the farthest limits of greater Casablanca.

Almost every week contractors turn up, offering me fistfuls of cash in return for parting with my great love. Some of them have promised to transform the house and gardens into a Caliph's House pleasure dome devoted to my book, while secretly conspiring to knock her down, like all the rest.

Whatever the story they tell, the contractors invariably arrive at the door, tape measures in hand – like an undertaker in a Spaghetti Western who measures the cowboy for his coffin before a duel.

The most wonderful thing about publishing *The Caliph's House* has been the fragments of Dar Khalifa's story that were revealed little by little in the months and years after the book's release. I received dozens of emails and hand-written letters from people who had attended parties there. Some described masked jamborees, while others spoke of diplomatic dinners held for royalty, literary dinners, and even séances.

The incoming messages were not limited to Dar Khalifa.

A favourite was sent to me by an elderly American couple, who had lived in Tangier in the summer of 1969. They'd known my grandfather, and had taken the disgraced psychologist Timothy Leary to meet him. Their description of that moment in Tangier's protracted timeline was a blur of kaleidoscopic colour… a dominion of beatniks, travellers, hippies, and fugitives.

By far the most moving message I received in the wake of publishing *The Caliph's House* came from a French gentleman named Pierre. His parents had purchased the property in the 1950s, and he had grown up at the house, just as my own children did.

In a message that touched me in the most profound way, he described an ordinary afternoon like any other. His little sister was out in the garden, playing on her swing.

All of a sudden, the tranquillity was shattered by an explosion.

The family ran out to see what had happened.

To their horror and dismay, Pierre's sister was lying dead on the grass. Dynamite had been being used in the small quarry behind the house, sending a fusillade of rocks in all directions.

Pierre described how his parents carried the child's frail body into Dar Khalifa and how it was laid on ice in the sitting room. A thousand times since, I have stood right there, and done my best to imagine the scene, and the incalculable depth of their sorrow.

Having heard Pierre's story, I was confused.

Why hadn't anyone ever told us of the tragedy?

One afternoon soon after, I found myself in the kitchen chatting with Zohra. She'd been telling me how two of her children had died in infancy in the *bidonville*. I asked why she had never told us about that part of her life before, just as no one had ever spoken about the death of the little French girl.

Zohra looked up from the pot of soup she was stirring on the stove.

Staring into space, she said:

'We never speak of such things because they don't bring

back those we have loved.'

From: *The Caliph's House*

# The Flying Carpet

GREAT TRAVEL WRITING is all about evoking an atmosphere of adventure. But more than that, it's about storytelling plain and simple.

Far too many works of travel slip into obscurity because the writing is lacklustre, dated, or downright dull. Trawl the shelves of the London Library and you'll find miles and miles of books that are all but forgotten. And many of them deserve to be left there – deep underground.

Yet from time to time you come across an author whose work is a beacon of originality. The American adventurer, Richard Halliburton, whose life was snuffed out at far too early an age, was one such writer.

Although his work has a small but devoted following, his books warrant a far greater readership – and are the kind of travel literature that have withstood the test of time, and continue to inspire the youth to achieve.

Born in 1900, in Brownsville, Tennessee, Halliburton was always destined for great things. His family were wealthy enough to send him to Princeton, a springboard into the Ivy League lifestyle so fêted in the rip-roaring twenties.

A contemporary of Hemmingway, the young Halliburton had none of the melancholy and all of the passion. Brimming with charm, good looks and natural charisma, he was the kind of man to whom both men and women were drawn.

While others were languishing on the terrors of the Great War, Halliburton was setting about making a name for himself by crisscrossing crumbling empires by any means possible. Making use of the media with impressive foresight, one can only imagine the heights to which he'd have soared given the technology we all take for granted today.

To grasp Halliburton's celebrity, it helps to understand the time in which he lived. His playground was the world caught in a no-man's land between the wars. The British Empire still ruled the seas; ferocious tribes inhabited the endless African plains and the seething jungles of the Amazon and Borneo; and motor cars were a *jeu du jour* for tin-pot dictators, maharajahs, and for anyone else with the means to afford them.

But most of all, it was a time in which great marvels were still to be found, and in which new technologies suddenly put great holy grails of worldwide travel within reach.

And there was no piece of machinery more revolutionary in the arena of modern exploration than the aeroplane.

A pioneer, a trailblazer, not to mention a media junkie, Halliburton understood the power of making a splash. In the vein of *Ripley's Believe It Or Not*, he tantalized his readers with jaw-dropping accounts of intrigue, exploration, and awe.

Of the handful of books he published, there's one that stands out as a monument to the time in which he lived, as much as it is a chronicle of everything Halliburton stood for. *The Flying Carpet* is a rare and enthusing tale of *Boy's Own* bravado. It's one of those books that stays with you, not so much because of the intoxicating roll-call of adventure, but because of the frantic sizzle of the tale.

Halliburton may have been thirty but he was gripped as

ever by the raw enthusiasm of a twelve-year-old. Longing to once again be, as he put it, a 'footloose vagabond', he searched for an aeroplane capable of crossing deserts and jungles, oceans and seas. With hardly any preparation and almost no background knowledge of flight, he bought one on the spur of the moment – a Stearman biplane. Shiny and small, with an open cockpit, he christened it the *Flying Carpet*.

The only thing needed now was a pilot.

By a stroke of luck he was introduced to a young Stanford graduate named Moye Stephens, who was employed flying passengers over the Rockies. Sharing the same lust for daredevil adventure, Stephens readily agreed to pilot them both on a circumnavigation of the globe – 'to all the outlandish places on earth'. He was promised no pay, but unlimited expenses.

His only question was when they were to leave.

'In half an hour,' Halliburton replied casually.

And, pulling him to the door, they did.

The journey was the kind of feat that people are drawn to recreate today, but with a rigid safety net of support. And yet the alluring thing about Halliburton and Stephens's epic flight was the absolute lack of safety, and the child-like zigzagging of wonders of the old world.

Halliburton was dead set on visiting Timbuctoo first. Lured by the mystery of the name and by its seeming inaccessibility, all he knew was that it was 'somewhere in Africa'.

To reach it, they traversed the United States eastwards

from California, headed south through Europe, and into the mysterious hinterland of Morocco.

Soaring high above the Atlas, they climbed to fifteen thousand feet to avoid pot shots from the tribesmen eager to bring down a shiny little plane like theirs.

And then, laden with extra fuel, they began the gruelling flight southwards, with the endless dunes of the Sahara laid out in a vast ocean beneath. Warned time and again about sand storms, but taking no notice, they flew headlong into one after the next, their faces and the *Flying Carpet* rasped raw.

Causing immense excitement as it came to land at Timbuctoo, the little biplane assured the two Americans immediate celebrity. They were received by Père Yakouba, the so-called 'White Monk of Timbuctoo' – the first of many intriguing locals they encountered.

Flying on eastwards, they reached the Algerian Sahara, where they were welcomed into the fold of the French Foreign Legion, at Colomb Bechar. Amazing those they met with acrobatics, and tall tales of their journey so far, they flew back up to Europe.

In an era in which travel was far more leisurely an activity, they took off and landed where they liked, *when* they liked. Reaching Italy through the Simplon Pass, they made a beeline for Venice, where they spent a month.

Then they wondered where next. Halliburton wrote:

Once more we unrolled our world map. Moye suggested Berlin. I voted for Malta. We compromised on Constantinople. A few hours later the *Flying Carpet* and its crew were in the air. Our first stop was Vienna. Then to Budapest – to Belgrade – to Bucharest – through storms, across plains, over mountains – on to Constantinople and the Golden Horn.

On and on they flew…

Across Turkey, down through the Holy Land, to Cairo and the Pyramids, over the Nabatean ruins of Petra, and eastwards over the great basalt desert to Baghdad.

The frequency with which they landed must have reflected the trying conditions of low-altitude, open-cockpit flight. Yet, always gung-ho in style, Halliburton's writing brushes aside the air-sickness from what must have been rollercoaster flights.

But their eagerness to land was inspired, too, by a genuine delight in witnessing new realms. At a time when the globe was not yet homogenized by mass media and equally mass travel, Halliburton and Stephens observed first-hand the last vestiges of the old world order.

And wherever they went, their celebrity status was enough for the doors of palaces, monasteries, and jungle longhouses to be flung open for them.

No one, it seemed, wanted to be left out.

In Baghdad, they took the young Crown Prince Ghazi up for a ride; and, in Persia, they carried aloft daughter of the Shah, Princess 'Flower-of-the-Morning'. While in Persia, they helped out the stricken German aviatrix, Elly Beinhorn, who was flying solo around the world, and had just arrived from Timbuctoo. Aged just twenty-three, she was the same age as Stephens. She must have outlived all the other early pilots for whom longevity was at odds with their sport. She finally passed away aged 100, in 2007.

Halliburton was a great believer in wonders of the world. He understood that associating his expedition with great landmarks would guarantee the media exposure he so desired. Soaring over the Taj Mahal was a natural way to hit the headlines back home, as was the daring flight in the shadows of Mount Everest.

A devoted aficionado of George Mallory, who had perished on that mountain seven years before, Halliburton was desperate to do a fly-by in some kind of tribute. Risking life and limb, and freezing solid in the ultra-thin air, they managed, with Halliburton taking the first aerial shots of the mountain with his camera.

The episode is Halliburton's style at its best. He wrote:

> And then Everest itself, indescribably magnificent, taunting the heavens with its gleaming crown. Her precipice, her clinging glacier shield, her royal streamer forever flying eastward from the throne, her court of gods and demons, her hypnotic, deadly beauty… what incomparable glory crowns this Goddess Mother of all mountains!

Of all the characters and encounters, my very favourite comes a little further, once they had traversed Burma,

Indochina, and arrived at the seething, steaming jungles of Borneo. There, they found the fabulously eccentric English aristocrat the Ranee Lady Sylvia Brooke, whose husband ruled Sarawak, a principality the size of Britain, peopled with Dayak headhunters. The author of a remarkable book herself (entitled *Queen of the Headhunters*), they took her up and did acrobatics over the jungles that were her home.

An astounding success, the Flying Carpet Expedition helped make Halliburton a household name across the United States. The adventure supposedly cost him $50,000, but he recouped twice that in media deals – a huge amount for the time.

The project's popularity came about because of the intoxicating cocktail it contained. There was adventure in great measure, humour and a smattering of history. But, more importantly, there was the overwhelming sense that just about anyone could follow Halliburton's lead and embark on a madcap escapade just like him.

And, for me, that's the great attraction of all his work.

A fresh, young-faced layman with no technical experience, Richard Halliburton surfed a tidal wave of enthusiasm and good old get-up-and-go. He wasn't trying to impress with ground-breaking hypotheses, or by discovering far-flung lands. Rather, his writing was a sympathetic lens through which ordinary people could experience the extraordinary world in which they lived.

But most of all, it was storytelling *par excellence*.

From: *The Flying Carpet*

## The Glorious Adventure

THERE WAS BETWEEN the wars a faint aperture of time in which great marvels were still to be found.

These holy grails of travel were made reachable through new technologies, and by the boldness and grit of an intrepid band of women and men – a new breed of explorer.

Until then, travel chronicles had been dominated by the great nineteenth-century adventurers. Mostly men, they were towering figures of Victorian celebrity – names like Burton, Barth, Livingstone and Stanley. Their accounts of subjugating natives and hoisting the flag for colonial rule were at best terse and at worst unreadable, by today's standards at least.

But with the slaughter of the Great War gone, the Roaring Twenties were a gateway to a new realm. Touched with frivolity, it was a time to assuage the pain of battle and to uplift the sunken hearts of armchair explorers the world over.

The result was a new kind of work – the birth of the modern travel book. Quests in their own right, these accounts were less about empire or life-and-death exploration, and more about engaging the reader through passionate description.

On the eastern shores of the Atlantic we like to imagine that to be a worthy adventurer you have to be a European as well. But nothing could be further from the truth. Leading the field in this genre of new romanticism was a zealous young American named Richard Halliburton.

Born into a middle-class home in Brownsville, Tennessee

at the start of 1900, Halliburton was a frail youth who suffered from a heart murmur. Despite an enthusiasm for the outdoors and for sport, he was confined to bed for months at a time in childhood, and even attended the legendary Battle Creek Sanitarium of self-styled nutritionist John Harvey Kellogg.

Putting his clinical confinement to use, Halliburton devoured every work of geography and exploration available. Yearning for a time when he could break free, he longed to experience the wild lands of which he had read. A romantic through and through, he had been weaned on the Classics, a fabulous backdrop and a blend of fact and fantasy *par excellence*.

Indefatigable, eloquent, and rip-roaringly upbeat, Halliburton was intensely alluring as a character. Soon after graduating from Princeton, he was well on his way to achieving the celebrity he so desired. Inspired by the intellect of Oscar Wilde, and the glamour of Rudolf Valentino, he was himself a dandy of the time. Impeccably dressed, exquisitely groomed, charming and ambitious, it's easy to imagine him as a player in the Great Gatsby world of the inter-war years.

For me, Halliburton's most intoxicating quality was the effortlessness with which he embarked upon a quest. Respectful, yet deaf to his detractors, he followed his gut, and used the media to his advantage right from the start. Certainly, the old guard wrote him off as whimsical, but Richard Halliburton was a man who grasped the pulse of the time better than almost anyone else alive.

The 1920s were about recuperation, a return to the

serenity of the Classical world that had been so obliterated from common culture on Flanders' fields. By understanding this – and by adoring it – Halliburton rose to astonishing fame. By the thirties he was a household name across America.

Daring, jovial, and eccentric, reports of his expeditions filled the news reels of the time, to the delight of a generation of youth. His *Boy's Own* style of adventure leaps off the page, the kind of writing that can't fail to enthuse, inspiring as much as it does entertain. Relying on fledgling aviation much of the time, and never fearful of terrible danger, Halliburton broke new ground, soaring high above wonders that other travellers had only skirted from the ground.

As far as he was concerned, the world was his giant playground, one still unscathed by mass tourism, political correctness, or industry. In this sunset of empire, the suave and fearless young Halliburton could do no wrong. Fêted by columnists and swooned over by adoring young women – and men – he was in a league of his own.

First published in 1928, *The Glorious Adventure* was Halliburton's second book. It came hot on the heels of *The Royal Road to Romance*, an amalgamation of disparate travels through Europe, North Africa, Central Asia and the Far East.

In scope, *The Glorious Adventure* is certainly far less wieldy than any of the other Halliburton travelogues. By choosing Homer's Odyssey as his theme – his great childhood love – he embarks on a journey to the theatre in which ancient Greece was played out. Lyrical, light-hearted and passionate without end, the book must have been a hymn to thousands of young men about to be hammered by the Wall Street crash of 1929.

His reasoning to leave is as spirited as the quest itself. He wrote:

> Suddenly I became bored and impatient with everything I had and was: bored with people, bored with knowledge. I realized I didn't want knowledge. I only wanted my senses to be passionately alive, and my imagination fearlessly far-reaching. And instead, I felt I was sinking into a slough of banality. Adventure! Adventure! *That* was the escape; *that* was the remedy.

Seeking out the land of the Lotus Eaters, the Cyclops's cave, Circe's lair, and Mount Olympus, home of the gods, Halliburton satiates his need for adventure and his infatuation for the Classical world. Fast-paced and furious, the writing style froths with verve and, at times, exhausts even the most devoted fan.

Enamoured by the life and legacy of the English war poet, Rupert Brooke, Halliburton seeks out his grave on the Greek island of Skyros. It was there the poet had expired in his prime from fever whilst en route to Gallipoli. But it was another English poet – Lord Byron – who provided the inspiration for the greatest feat of the journey. Following his lead, Halliburton succeeded in swimming the Hellespont, the brutal current almost drowning him.

As his meteoric career progressed, and as he crisscrossed

the planet, Richard Halliburton became one of the most travelled men alive. Always longing for adventure, one gets the feeling he also longed to be remembered, cognizant of the fact it would take one slip up, or act of God, to end it all.

And ultimately, Halliburton's daredevil brand of travel ran out of luck. Not yet forty, he had embarked on his most hazardous adventure – The Sea Dragon Expedition, in 1939. Having commissioned a Chinese junk in Hong Kong, he intended to cross the Pacific to San Francisco.

Following a catalogue of teething problems, the craft set out.

After three weeks at sea, and aloft mountainous waves, they sent their final radio dispatch.

Neither the *Sea Dragon*, Halliburton, nor the crew, were ever heard of again.

To disappear on the trail of a glorious quest is surely the secret dream of any travel writer. But to vanish in one's prime – with years of accomplishments still unfulfilled – is our great loss.

Richard Halliburton deserves the celebrity he so enjoyed, and to be remembered as an inspiration from the nascent age of modern travel. His was a time of good manners, genteel delivery and, most of all, of impassioned values. It was an era of biplanes, tramp steamers, and of vast open-topped vehicles, a world in which most of humanity had not yet been exposed to the trappings of the industrial age.

And, of course, all too soon, the technology that made such travel possible for one made it possible for all, with a result of a homogenized global culture – something

Halliburton would surely have despised.

As I see it, what he stood for was as important as what he achieved. A new romantic without equal, Halliburton's *joie de vivre* and gung-ho attitude was itself a catalyst that rallied a generation to go out and seek marvels of their own. And, as such, his legacy is not only poignant, but a tangible gift that continues to inspire today.

From: *The Glorious Adventure*

ON A LONG journey through the Arab world, I once found myself at a desert encampment, a perfectly full moon casting its silvery aspect over the clusters of tents.

Squatting close to the fire, I was doing my best to warm my hands when one of my Bedouin hosts approached. He greeted me, gave thanks for such a splendid night, and said:

'If only we could transmit this moment into the minds of others.'

'Who do you mean?'

'To the people of the Occident.'

'But they know of Arabia, or at least a form of it,' I answered.

The Bedouin warmed his hands in silence, his long, lean silhouette motionless like a blackened statue.

'In the West, people think they know the East because they've seen it on television. But they're missing what matters.'

'And what's that?'

The Bedouin turned a fraction, his face illuminated by the flames.

'The essence,' he said.

For twenty years I have turned those two words over in my mind, doing my best to understand them, to appreciate their significance.

The more I've considered them, the more I've perceived their profundity. The Bedouin traveller at that desert caravanserai couldn't have perceived the way things are with sharper insight.

The essence.

That's all that really matters.

As my children, Ariane and Timur, have progressed through school and entered the world, I have often observed the twists and turns of their education. I've pondered what they were taught, and why, just as I've revisited my own education a generation ago.

Looking at it all, I have been continually struck at the linear approach to learning that the Occident provides. They celebrate it, of course, singing their own praises from the rooftops, awarding themselves hollow honours, and insisting that theirs is the only way to achieve real understanding.

My journeys in the Orient – a realm I would argue begins at Istanbul, and stretches to the remote tracts of the Japanese archipelago – have taught me about learning from the inside out.

A Persian friend and I were once discussing philosophy, and the state of the world.

Her name was Farzana, and she'd moved to North Africa in the hope, as she put it, 'of smelling a different wind'.

Farzana had an infectious smile, and always seemed to be smiling, even when she was not. The muscles of her face were taut and strong from all the smiling, and her teeth were blindingly white, as though polished specially so as to make the smile even more dazzling than it might have been.

I can't quite remember what prompted Farzana into making the comment she did, only that it left her mouth and touched my ears.

'The West operates in the most obvious way,' she said.

'Does it?'

'Yes.'

'How does that change things?'

'In every imaginable way.'

We were sitting on the beach, a makeshift picnic strewn over a sandy rug, the winter sun lowering itself towards the waves.

Farzana picked up an apple, threw it up into the air, and caught it in her small, delicate hand.

'In the West, they tell you about things,' she said. 'If they are talking about apples, they explain the fruit's history, how they were developed, and cross-bred. They'd tell you, too, how apples are good for the health, how many calories they have, and how to grow them best.'

'And what's wrong with that?'

'Nothing at all… except that it doesn't teach you about the essence of the fruit.'

My mind was transported back to the Bedouin encampment.

'You mean we should be considering apples, and everything else, from the inside out?'

Farzana bit into the apple, chewed in silence, then swallowed.

'In the East we'd never be so straight-forward,' she said. 'Instead of all the obvious nonsense, we'd tell you about how the apple tasted, the difference it made to our culture, and we'd tell you stories galore about apples.'

I wondered aloud why the West was so different to the East.

'If you watch how children learn,' Farzana said, 'you'll see that kids never approach anything at all in a linear way. That's the very last way they'd ever do anything.'

'You mean that they dive in at the middle, and feel their way all around something until they've got enough to piece together?'

Farzana flashed her blinding white grin.

'Exactly,' she said. 'In the East we were never separated from this method of doing things. The result is that we learn, and function, in a completely different way.'

'How?'

'Through fragments of knowledge and information which, when grouped together or overlapped, form a magical tapestry – a tapestry that's the most powerful learning matrix ever devised.'

In approaching *The Middle East Bedside Book*, I did so with an Oriental mindset.

The last thing I wanted was to compile a book that would tell people about the East from A to Z. My ambition was to provide the kind of teaching quilt that Farzana had spoken about – formed of mismatching fragments.

I'm not going to pretend that all the fragments in this book fit together perfectly. My hope is that, as there's such a variety – and the occasional 'curve ball' – a reader's understanding of the material will be challenged and stretched.

Nothing interests me less than a linear approach to anything.

Anyone who's read books with my name on the spine will find a common theme of Zigzag Think running through the millions of words I've published. The way I see it, we can only push ahead by observing problems, ideas, and information by considering the essence – not by the standard appreciation from start to end.

A few years ago I was going through some box files from the archive of my grandfather, The Sirdar Ikbal Ali Shah. The author of more than seventy books, a diplomat, advisor to heads of state, and world traveller at a time when virtually no one went anywhere, he was a veritable bridge between West and East.

Amongst his papers I found a note, typed out on a manual typewriter.

It read:

> The Occident is a little boy, and the Orient a wizened old man. The child believes he knows everything, that he's an expert, even though he's so terribly raw. You can do your best to teach him, but he has to learn through having the corners knocked away by the twists and turns of life. The East is rounded like the pebbles on a riverbed. They're so smooth that you cannot fail to be mesmerized by their journey. If the Occident is to mature to adulthood, it must first learn to stop babbling like a toddler, and listen like a sage.

My earnest hope is that the pages of *The Middle East Bedside Book* will present a zigzagging patchwork quilt of know-how – that tells a story of its own from the inside out.

From: *The Middle East Bedside Book*

# The Reason to Write

I WAS BORN into a family of writers.

My father, aunt, both grandfathers, grandmother, sisters, and me – each one of us has walked the same path. A path that has at times reduced us to madness, just as it's sustained us with triumphant success.

Since the earliest days of childhood, I was introduced to the world through an author's eyes. Almost everything ever explained to me was explained from a writer's point of view – as if I were pitted against those who were not in the know.

Dozens of my parents' friends were writers, too – some the most successful literary names of their age – among them J. D. Salinger, Doris Lessing, and Robert Graves. Convening at our home in the lush English countryside, they would listen to my father, the author and thinker Idries Shah, taking more than what was merely spoken.

Looking back, it was as though they were members of a secret fellowship, one that I myself was eventually destined to join.

When I close my eyes and think back to my childhood, the overriding memory is not a sight, a smell, or even a taste.

But a sound.

The sound of a manual typewriter clattering away downstairs in my father's study.

*Clack! Clack! Clack! Clack!*

Like a knight in shining armour doing battle with a dragon, it was a tumultuous and intoxicating riot of noise. The clatter of typewriter keys was far more than the sound of an author tapping out books.

It was the musical score to my youth.

On the rare occasions the clatter stopped, I'd freeze, swallow hard with fear, and tiptoe downstairs to see what was wrong. My father would be hunched over his old Triumph machine, a fistful of pages held up to his face. Wincing, wheezing, his head framed in cigar smoke curls, he'd be lost in an enchanted realm – a state of mind.

I've come to know it as 'The Magic Zone'.


My father once gave a lecture at an Ivy League university in New England.

Listening to a recording of it, I can picture the scene perfectly. When he'd been introduced, he informed the students he was going to talk for an hour, just as he'd been asked to do. Then, smiling wryly, he said:

'But first I am going to let you into a little secret. I'm probably not supposed to tell you this, but I will anyway, because it's an example of the way I regard the world and everything in it.'

The students glanced up in genuine interest.

'Now that I have your attention,' my father went on, 'I'll tell you the secret… Although I'm scheduled to talk to you for an hour, I could do the talk in three and a half minutes. I could even do it in two minutes, if you listened hard. But I'm not going to – even though I'd probably be the most popular visiting professor ever to lecture here. The reason is because the Occidental society in which we live confuses container with content. If I were to say everything I had to deliver in three and a half minutes, the faculty which is covering my fee would regard me as a fraudster.'

As promised, my father went on to deliver the entire lecture, and was applauded long and hard at the end. The central theme – of 'Container and Content' – shaped the university lectures he delivered all over the world, as well as many of his books, most notably *The Book of the Book*.

'Container and Content' is an idea on which I myself was weaned.

In all my time hunting for examples of back-to-front thinking, one looms larger to me than any other. Indeed, in the same way my father might have delivered his lecture in a couple of minutes, I could pass on the entire meat of this book in a single line.

But I'm not going to, even though it would save on paper, and would give you more time to lavish on eating ice cream, lying on the beach, or provide extra hours to spend on your own writing.

Rather than condensing my material to a line, I'll shorten it to the bare bones of what it's all about:

There are all kinds of writers out there, writing all kinds of work.

My key point centres around the way things are, and the way things ought to be.

They're quite different – like two paths that once ran as one, before forking sharply away in different directions. My mission is to get the paths back to how they were supposed to be – running together like a lovely towpath following the twists and turns of a river… a towpath that did service to the writers first, and to everyone else second.

To understand what I'm saying, I must to take you back to how the great scheme of things were shaped before they went off-kilter. So please bear with me and allow me a little poetic licence.

In 'the olden times' (as my kids used to call anything that happened a long time ago), there weren't many publishers as we know them today. Most of the time an author would write a book, then give it to a printer who would typeset it by hand, print it, and knock it back to the writer, who would go out and sell it to his chums.

Little by little the system took off.

The authors realized they could write a lot more if they didn't have to spend so much time selling their work. So they gave it to guys hanging around on street corners to sell on their behalf.

Time passed, and the street hawkers made money from peddling the writers' fresh work. They got themselves kiosks, and eventually fully fledged bookshops. Even though back then books weren't books as we know them. You see, until the 1830s a book was sold in its raw state – without covers as we have them today. The posh people (who were buying most of the books) didn't want covers anyway. They would send anything they bought to their binder to have it bound in the uniform livery of their private library.

Years dragged on.

The writers wrote, the booksellers sold, and all was generally good. By now some booksellers were doing so well that they branched out. Instead of just selling printed work given to them by writers, they started representing them, too. Note: it was the booksellers who did the branching out and not the printers – which surely would have made more sense.

A little further along, the bookseller-publishers were doing so well from the arrangement, they started to look for gaps in the market so they could clean up all the more. They grabbed hold of writers whose work was well received, and offered them cold hard cash in return for being locked into publishing contracts.

If I could go back to any time in history, it would be that moment.

The moment the first greedy, self-important publisher got an ingenuous author to sign away his or her rights and – more importantly – to sign away their control.

As you can imagine from my tone, my wish to time-travel was so I could break up the meeting, rip the contract into confetti, and hightail it out of there with the writer.

But I can't travel back in time, so we're stuck with a reality path that became a normality path – the path in which writers are told what to write by publishers, or at least how to write it. I know there are exceptions, and not all publishers are ghouls, but the vast majority of them are and always have been.

Of course they are.

Why?

Because the existing model of publishing is like the standard red-light districts I've seen throughout my travels. A sordid underworld of brothels, hustlers, and pimps. I've seen pimps wearing some very flash outfits and sporting plenty of gold, but they're still pimps, just as the brothels are always brothels, despite what the sign says.

In the same way, I've known publishers who have *crème de la crème* offices, and who lay on lavish lunches with *foie gras* and champagne, but that doesn't make them any less pimpy than they are.

The bad news: Things are back to front, because they got flipped way back when.

The good news: Everything's going to be just fine.

'*Really?*' I hear you asking.

## YES! YES! YES!

I can see you hovering over the page, eager to know how I can be so sure. The answer is a single word:

## TECHNOLOGY

In the same way technology got authors into a bind in the first place, it's going to free them from the shackles of bondage.

I have a lot to say about writers and writing, about agents and publishers, about the way it is, and the way it could and should be.

As anyone who's had the misfortune of sitting next to me at a dinner party will know, I can rant on for hours, venting strong views like scalding jets shot out from a geyser. I suspect my fellow dinner guests imagine my opinions were dreamt up that very day. But they weren't. Like a baton passed on from one generation to the next, the way I understand authorship was laid down over an entire century.

One of my earliest memories is being six years old, sent from the playroom down to one of the formal salons at our home in the English countryside, Langton House. The Durbar was the former billiard room, dating to the time when Robert Baden-Powell – founder of the Boy Scouts – grew up there just like I did.

Sweeping in, dressed in a flowing 1970s kaftan, my mother ordered me to be on 'Best Behaviour', a phrase that meant sitting up ramrod straight and speaking only when spoken to. To me, 'Best Behaviour' meant being trussed up in a tight Oriental costume and having my hair brushed very roughly.

But most of all, it meant someone important was about to arrive.

On that day when I was six, an American gentleman strolled in through the front door.

I remember him more for what he was not than what he was. He was not loud, brash, or ostentatious, like the other Best Behaviour guests. Rather, he was exceedingly soft-spoken, gentle, and kind. When he left, my father exclaimed he was 'a truly great man'.

I asked who he was.

'He's a writer.'

'What is his name?'

'Mr. Salinger.'

'Does he write children's books?' I asked.

'He writes for everyone,' my father replied. 'At the same time, he writes for himself.'

'Why does he write?'

My father considered the question, his brow furrowing as he did so.

'Mr. Salinger writes because he *must* write,' he said. 'He can't help it... he can't stop.'

'Baba, what would happen if Mr. Salinger stopped writing?' I asked.

'If J. D. Salinger stopped writing, he'd turn to stone,' my father said.

From: *The Reason to Write*

# The Story of Morocco

Six years ago I received a phone call from an elderly American lady with a shrill voice, and a chest that sounded as though it was clattering with multiple strings of beads.

In the short conversation, she informed me she was a veteran TV producer, that her work was the stuff of legend, and that I'd been recommended by a billionaire, an ambassador, and a king.

'Recommended for what?' I asked.

'Recommended for the project.'

'Which project?'

'The project to end all projects – *The Story of Morocco*!'

The following week I happened to be in New York for a book tour, and was invited to a plush brownstone apartment where the lady, Lucy Jarvis, lived. In the years since, I've found myself wondering how I would ever describe her.

A good place to start would be with a line of description of her salon.

The room was festooned with Oriental furniture – a magnificent Chinese lacquered screen and matching cabinet; cloisonné vases, and lamps adorned with the finest gold tracery I've seen outside of a museum. But it wasn't the furniture that caught my attention, so much as the photographs.

There were dozens of them.

Each one, framed in silver, showed Lucy with a head of state, a Hollywood icon, or someone so famous that you couldn't help but do a double take. There was Lucy with

the Reagans, Lucy with the Dalai Lama, and with Mother
Theresa; Lucy arm in arm with British royalty, with Robert
Redford, with Elizabeth Taylor, and even with JFK.

As if having positioned herself in the right spot so as to
garner maximum effect, Lucy Jarvis was standing against
the Chinese screen, a flock of wild swans in flight behind
her head. Her back ramrod straight, she was large-boned
and elegant, and I assumed she was in her late seventies.
As I drew close to shake her hand, her mouth erupted into
a smile, like an automaton. Framed in a prodigious layer
of fire-red lipstick, the same smile had wooed royalty and
celebrities the world over.

Once pleasantries were over, Lucy ushered me to a
seat and reminded me that I'd been recommended by a
billionaire, an ambassador, and a king. I got the sense the
information was repeated more so that Lucy could allude
to the fact that she knew a billionaire, an ambassador, and a
king, and less because it was actually relevant.

I enquired delicately about the project.

'I want to make a grand documentary about Morocco,'
she said. 'A showcase of the culture, the traditions, and the
ancient heritage.'

'Where do I fit in?'

'You will write it, and I won't take no for an answer!'

My face clenched tight, and I said:

'Won't you?'

'No I won't!'

'How d'you know I'm the right man for the job?'

Lucy swallowed hard. Her gaze lowered onto the Ming

226

table, then by gradual degrees up onto my face.

'I know because of experience,' she said. 'I've had a seventy-five-year career.'

'Were you a child star?'

Lucy blinked slowly, indicating she hadn't been.

'Go on, guess my age.'

I flinched, as one always does when put in such a precarious situation.

'Seventy-five?'

'Ninety-seven,' she replied.

And so that's how I came to be sitting in the desert of Morocco's east with a ninety-seven-year-old film producer, scouting the kingdom in which I lived, in preparation for the documentary to end all documentaries – *The Story of Morocco*.

Lucy had climbed up onto a camel so that a photograph could be taken and sent to everyone she knew. Now fatigued, she lashed out at the team, of which I was a reluctant member.

If truth be told, we were all reluctant members, all wondering how we had been coaxed and cajoled into taking part, even though funding hadn't been mentioned.

During the downtime, the others and I shared fragments of the hyperbole that had lured us from our ordinary lives and onto the project.

One of the team, a veteran filmmaker, said:

'In wooing me, she pulled out all the stops. It was the wooing that every filmmaker dreams of – the wooing to end all woos.'

When the reconnaissance around Morocco was at an end, I wrote an introduction to the film I thought Lucy was hoping to make.

The text follows below.

At the same time, I promised myself to have nothing more to do with her ever again – a decision I chalked down to gut feelings.

In the first week of February this year, the same gut feeling prompted me to type the name 'Lucy Jarvis' into Google.

A moment later, I discovered that a week previously the inimitable producer had departed for happier hunting grounds...

...aged a hundred and two.


The ancient labyrinth of Fès is a place of secrets and of mysteries, a realm that's changed little in a thousand years and more.

So narrow are the telescoping streets that cars can't breach the medina, the old city. Instead, the interwoven lanes and passages – some as slender as a barrel's length – are still plied day and night by legions of pack mules, unchanged since antiquity.

Laden with everything from furniture and silks, to cases of Coca-Cola and flat-screen TVs, they push through the densest hustle and bustle, a last surviving fragment of *A Thousand and One Nights*.

Stall-keepers splash water over the steps of their shops, making ready for the brisk morning trade. Clutching buckets, mothers and daughters venture out to the nearby *hammam*, the communal steam baths, still used by one and all. A procession of donkeys clip-clop their way uphill from the tanneries, burdened with great bales of damp leather hides. Live chickens are weighed out on a butcher's scales, and ripe figs are exchanged for a handful of coins.

Amid it all, comes the *muezzin*'s voice calling the faithful to prayer, from the minaret of a mosque, half as old as time.

A stone's throw from the market is an imposing arched doorway. In its shade is a cluster of storytellers, regaling passers-by with tales of Aladdin and Sindbad, of treasures and princesses, of sorcerers, and of carpets that fly.

On the other side of the doorway lies an imposing courtyard.

The walls and floor are laid with intricate hand-cut mosaics, the warm air soothed by the sound of water issuing forth from fountains at each end. This is the al-Karaouine, founded in 859 AD, the oldest surviving university on earth.

The courtyard may seem a million miles from the world we know, but it has directly affected all our lives. An ancient crucible of scholarship, al-Karaouine was once part of a vast network of learning – linking Cairo, Damascus, and Andalusian Spain to Bukhara, Samarkand, and even Timbuktu.

Through the Middle Ages, when Europe was embroiled in endless conflicts and wars, Fès was a powerhouse of knowledge and new understanding. Taking the incomplete sciences of the Classical world, its scholars were part of a Golden Age of Learning, one that formed the basis of our own scientific dominion.

From its cloisters came astonishing breakthroughs in medicine and metallurgy, in chemistry and botany, in astronomy and mathematics – advances that filtered northward to Europe and beyond. The innovations have influenced every sphere of the world in which we live.

Without Fès, we would have no glass in our windows, no motorcars or computers, no vaccinations or printed books. There would be no satellites or space rockets either, no iPads or smart phones, no IBM, Apple or Internet.

The cultural and religious heart of Morocco, Fès stood at the crossroads of transmission, when Europe was ravaged by feudalism and plague, and when the New World lay undiscovered.

Visit the Universities of Oxford or Cambridge today, and you find the same cloistered courtyard structures, inspired by the University of al-Karaouine.

Another legacy are the professorial gowns worn by university graduates the world over, a throwback to the medieval robes of Morocco – an attire still worn in the streets today.

At a time when relations between East and West have been strained to breaking point, it serves us well to remember how the Occident and Orient have been inseparable throughout history.

Know-how gleaned from the Classical world of the Romans and the Greeks was taken by the Arabs, honed, and adapted, at Fès and elsewhere, before being reintroduced back into Europe.

This cutting-edge knowledge was the spark that made the

European Renaissance possible. The knock-on effect was all-encompassing, and even led to the methods of navigation that allowed Europe to discover the New World.

For more than ten centuries, Morocco has stood at the cultural crossroads between Africa and Europe. Poised at the western-most edge of the Arab world, it looks out to the Americas, and up to Europe, its roots penetrating deep into Saharan sands.

A kingdom forged on ancient tradition and diehard values, it is a realm in which nothing is what it seems. Bathed in the folklore of *The Thousand and One Nights*, Moroccan culture is both superstitious and intertwined. Belief in jinn, sorcery, mysticism, and in the Evil Eye dies hard. Islam is the national religion, but religious tolerance is upheld as the mainstay of life.

A centre for geometric Islamic design, Morocco's craftsmen are still arranged in medieval guilds. Their secret know-how is passed down from one generation to the next through prolonged apprenticeships, the kind once found across Europe.

Presiding over the nation as Commander of the Faithful is King Mohammed VI, an ancestral monarch who's championed the rights of women and the dispossessed, and who continues to strive toward creating the most modern and tolerant land in the Islamic World.

The first country to publicly recognize the fledgling United States of America, the present King's ancestor Sultan Mohammed III signed the Moroccan-American Treaty of Friendship on 20 December 1777. Still very much in force, the treaty is regarded as the longest unbroken accord of Friendship between the United States and any foreign power. Indeed, in the northern Moroccan city of Tangier lies the American Legation, the only building on foreign soil registered as an American National Historic Landmark.

A journey through Morocco, crossroads between North and South, West and East, must consider the ancient elements of society, stark cultural landscapes, and the way in which the kingdom has defied recent trials and tribulations, afflicting much of the Arab world.

We shall visit the crumbling ruins of Volubilis, where the Romans had a major outpost south of the Mediterranean, two thousand years ago. And, we'll wend our way through the teeming lanes of Fès, through the magic market where sorcerers still buy ingredients for their spells, opening secret doors to both palaces and ordinary homes.

We will visit the workshops, in which artisans continue an unbroken chain of transmission, and the great cultural bastions from another time, and on to the desert encampments in which codes of chivalry and honour bind one man to the next, as they have done through human history.

And, of course, we will visit al-Karaouine, a focal point of learning that shapes our own cultures and our lives. We will venture across the mighty Atlas Mountains, snow-capped through even the hottest months, where rural life continues in villages untouched by the outside world. And we will journey on, through lush valleys irrigated by melting snows, down into the red desert – to the legendary Marrakech.

Taking in palaces and the ancient adobe walls, we will rub shoulders with storytellers and snake charmers, with Tuareg healers and with acrobats, with water-sellers, mystics and mendicants.

We will visit the Atlantic seaboard, too, where fishermen land a haul each morning, in waters that ebb and flow westward to the New World.

And we will beat a path deep into the desert, where herds of camel take refuge at distant caravanserais, around the campfires where an ageless folklore is told and retold.

Of course we shall visit the great urban centres as well, where old and new are overlaid – king among them Casablanca, a city championed in black and white by Bergman and Bogart seventy years ago.

Through our journey we will consider Morocco as a bridge between Occident and Orient, reflecting how the kingdom has influenced all our lives, and how it's remained defiant and strong.

Including experts on culture, folklore, and the arts as well as ordinary Moroccans, we will build up a picture of life, layer on layer. Listening to the sounds of Morocco, we'll learn its secrets, and take in the pungent scent of its mouth-watering cuisine.

But, most of all, we will glimpse the kingdom from the inside out, understanding it as Moroccans do, a mosaic-sized fragment at a time.

From: *The Story of Morocco*

# The Travels of Ibn Battutah

I REMEMBER CLEARLY the first time I heard the name Ibn Battutah. I was sitting on my grandfather's lap and I was three years old. It was the winter of 1969, and we were sitting in the garden of a little villa on Tangier's steep rue de la Plage. My grandfather, The Sirdar Ikbal Ali Shah, who was from Afghanistan, had moved to the northern Moroccan city after my grandmother died. So broken by loss, he had wanted to live in a place where they had never been together.

In the late sixties, Tangier was a melting pot of people unlike any other. Poised at the crossroads between Africa and Europe, it was jam-packed with ageing beatniks and tie-dye hippies, with draft-dodgers and fugitives, with poets, dreamers, and the dispossessed.

After a long pause, my grandfather motioned to the grass beneath his chair.

'You are very young,' he said, 'but you will grow and you will grow. And one day you will come to know the magic of this place, where we are sitting now.'

'Magic?' I said eagerly, because I loved magic.

'Yes, magic. It's the magic in a name tied to it.'

Shuffling round, I squinted at the old man's face. He smiled.

'The name is Ibn Battutah,' he said. 'Always remember it. Remember that name.'

'But why?'

'Because it will live on in your heart.'

Decades passed, and I almost forgot the name.

After all, our lives are awash with names and the achievements pinned to them, in a world with too many heroes. Then, one sleepless night half my life ago, I found myself trawling through a rack of tired old paperbacks at a friend's flat in Tokyo. I had been living on his floor for weeks, and had no books of my own.

A very worn volume caught my eye.

Or, rather, it caught my attention because of the way it felt. In the half-light it was rough to the touch, well loved, as if it had itself lived.

Jerking out the spine with the tip of my finger, I read the title: *The Travels of Ibn Battutah.*

Instantly, I was transported back to the patch of garden on rue de la Plage. Gazing down at me, the old man smiled, then nodded in approval. I opened the book, folded back the cover, and began a journey that has influenced every footstep I have taken ever since.

Years later, I came to know that my grandfather had chosen Tangier not only because of the lack of memories it held, but for its association with the greatest medieval traveller of all – Muhammad Ibn Ibrahim Ibn Battutah, a man who journeyed three times farther than Marco Polo. That he should spend the last decade of his life at this boisterous crossroads of West and East was more than fitting. It must have seemed like destiny. An expert on Islamic jurisprudence, a Sufi and a diplomat, my grandfather was above all a traveller. He once commented to my father that when his feet were not moving over the earth, his body was calcifying, each cell wasting into stone.

That Ibn Battutah was from Tangier is appropriate, just as it seems quite apposite that my grandfather had lived there in his retirement. Anyone who has ever felt the city's breeze on their face, or smelled the piercing scent of its orange blossom, has been inspired – inspired to venture to distant points of the compass. It's a city that bridges chasms of culture, a realm of infinite possibility and of youthful hope. And, just as it is a stepping stone for distant lands, Tangier is also a place to return to after a lifetime of adventure.

For twenty years and more I have roamed points east and west with Ibn Battutah as my companion. He's a hero of mine, a man charged with zeal, a savant and, most of all, a survivor. In my fascination for his life and for the *Rihla*, his astonishing masterwork, I have found that eventually all people and all places link up in a grand and enchanted matrix, the kind so common in the pages of *Alf Layla wa Layla, The Thousand and One Nights*.

My preoccupation with Ibn Battutah eventually led me to the inimitable Tim Mackintosh-Smith, albeit via a zigzag and circuitous route. In the late nineties we were both published by John Murray – at that time the finest, and possibly most eccentric, publishing house on the English literary scene. Over coffee at my first meeting there, my editor slid a copy of *Yemen: Travels in Dictionary Land* across the table. I asked about its author, said to be working on an ambitious trilogy about Battutah. The editor looked sheepish.

'There's no one else like him,' she said hesitantly.

'Is that a good thing or a bad thing?' I asked.

My editor bit her upper lip in a pause.

'I'm not quite sure,' she said.

I took the volume on Yemen home, and kept it on my desk as I struggled to write my own book, a rambling journey through the wilds of Ethiopia. Over weeks and months I read it, re-read it, lived with it, and analyzed its style.

And I cursed.

I cursed and I cursed, and I cursed and I cursed. *How could Tim Mackintosh-Smith be blessed with such damned genius – a genius that seemed to come so effortlessly?* His prose was a high plateau that every author aspires to reach. Yet most never even get close. Such was his skill, like that of a master swordsman, he could execute the simplest of moves and still never fail to impress.

Over the years since we were both at Murray's, I have taken Tim with me on journeys in some of the world's most obscure regions. And, through him, I like to think I have taken Ibn Battutah along as well. His trilogy appeared during the first decade of the new millennium: three books that were milestones in travel literature as much as they were studies of Battutah's journeys and his work.

The first was, of course, *Travels With a Tangerine*, a book that established Tim's unbridled enthusiasm for his subject, and a book charged with as many unlikely and beguiling characters as the *Rihla* itself. Charting the great traveller's route east from his homeland, it traces a meandering course through North Africa reaching Cairo, thence to Damascus, and, eventually, Constantinople.

From the first page, I smiled to myself, because the author

had (it seemed to me, anyway) used Battutah as a tool, a kind of Trojan horse, by which to educate his Occidental audience in the complexities of Arab society and its lore. An effective method, and an important one, it's something he continues in the subsequent parts of the trilogy, developing it further as he heads east.

Following on from *Tangerine*, the sequel volume – *The Hall of a Thousand Columns* – examines Ibn Battutah's trials and tribulations in the pastiche of lands and cultures that is India. Building on the achievement of the first book, although not relying on it, the journey is extraordinary in revealing how relatively little India has changed through centuries, at least from a cultural standpoint.

As for *Landfalls*, the concluding volume in the trilogy, it takes the reader through a varied miscellany of lands visited by the fourteenth-century adventurer. They include the Maldive archipelago, Sri Lanka, West Africa, Al-Andalus and, perhaps most significant of all – China. After all, it was the Prophet who said, 'Travel in search of knowledge, even though the journey take you to China.'

As for Tim Mackintosh-Smith's contribution, it is for me crystal clear. He has brought to life a character who had, until then, appeared rather dry and distant to Occidental readers. The secret weapon in his armoury is a blend of irresistible charm and good old-fashioned knowledge of the subject. In an age when authors are cajoled by some publishers to fast track their work to meet ever-tightening marketing deadlines, Tim's books are forged on a bedrock of top-notch scholarship and research.

Mackintosh-Smith is an intellectual, but the kind who has supreme value, because he can transcend the boundaries between academia and the world in which most of us reside. As someone who grew up with one foot in the Orient and the other in the Occident, I have come to appreciate how rare it is to find anyone who really understands both West and East. Orientals tend to be baffled by Western preoccupations and thought processes. And, all too often, Occidental society is hampered in making sense of the Orient because of ingrained misconceptions, and because of barriers in understanding the core values of Eastern culture.

Tim Mackintosh-Smith walks the line between the two in a way that few have done before him and, I am sure, not many will do after. He is an Arabist who has made his home in the Arab world for decades. In him, I am constantly reminded of my friend and mentor, Wilfred Thesiger.

Like Tim Mackintosh-Smith, Thesiger was fascinated with the Arab world, and keen not only to explore it, but to immerse himself in the interleaving layers, in a way that the great Victorian scholar-travellers like Burton and Doughty had done. For Thesiger, there was no point in being in a place if he was to be at odds with its people, or sequestered from them. He didn't want to hang about with expatriates, just as he didn't want the trappings of England he had left behind. Travel was, for him, a means to an end – a method of achieving total immersion.

I like to think the same goes for Mackintosh-Smith: that the years he has spent in Yemen have been quite indispensable. Without them he never would have slipped into the mindset necessary to complete the Ibn Battutah trilogy.

And it is that mindset which is such an enigma to the Occidental psyche. It seems so obvious, but reaching it – like the plateau of high prose for an author – is something that confounds intellectuals and travellers alike. Living in Morocco for the last handful of years and having travelled widely through many Arab lands, I have encountered all manner of 'Englishmen abroad'. Some of them don Arab dress, dine on the food, or even learn the dialect. But still they can't penetrate the mindset of Arab culture.

Tim Mackintosh-Smith is a clear exception.

Having given it a great amount of thought, I have come to the conclusion that it's related to the fact that he has gone about it in a back-to-front kind of way. Instead of struggling to hold something that cannot be held, he has done what any self-respecting Oriental would do – step back and allow the Arab mindset to enter him by a process of osmosis.

The result is an ability to treat the Orient on its own terms, to be a part of it, and to understand it from the inside out. For aficionados of Ibn Battutah, the consequences are profound. Through Tim Mackintosh-Smith's seemingly effortless expertise, humble admirers of *The Travels* like myself have a chance at glimpsing delights that were until now obscured.

Rather like a master gem-smith faceting a precious stone, Tim has excised distracting material in an effort to hone our attentions on the journeys themselves. Dazzling in its clarity, this pared-down version of the *Rihla* is an absolute joy to read. Whereas academics sometimes cling to challenged and discursive prose, Mackintosh-Smith is a champion of readability. As for the Folio Society's edition – it is exquisite in every way.

Last week I took the train north to Tangier from Casablanca, where I live. Arriving there just before dusk, I strolled down the promenade. There were couples hand in hand, gulls swooping and diving on the light breeze, the scent of late spring in the air.

Ibn Battutah was in my mind as I crossed the street and walked up rue de la Plage.

I paused at the iron door of my grandfather's villa – No. 71. It was at that precise spot that he breathed his last, a few days after revealing to his little grandson the legend of the great Arab traveller. At dusk one evening, while he was struggling to open the door, a reversing Coca-Cola truck knocked him down and killed him.

A little further up the hill, past the Grand Socco, I came to the café where my grandfather used to while away the mornings and afternoons. Ordering a cup of the ubiquitous *café noir*, I leant back in my chair and breathed in deep. There's nothing quite like Tangier to make one appreciate the zest for life, or the possibility of travel. The thought of it, of seizing the day, nudged me to fumble in my bag. I fished out my well-loved copy of the *Rihla*.

Opening it at random, as I like to do, I read:

The memory of my homeland moved me,
Together with affection for my people and friends,
And love for my country which for me is better
than all others,

A land where charms were hung upon me
Whose earth my skin first touched

Putting the book down on the tabletop, I sipped my coffee, looked out at the street.

'He came from this town,' said a husky voice.

I looked round to find the elderly waiter looming over me, a battered tea tray balanced between his hands.

'Who did?'

'The great traveller. Battutah.'

I smiled, nodded.

'I know he did.'

'Well, do you know why he came back to Tangier, after all those journeys?'

I frowned.

'Because when a man is from Tangier,' said the waiter slowly, 'he may journey as far as China, but his heart will be restless like a winter sea – restless until he comes home.'

From: *The Travels of Ibn Battutah*

## *Timbuctoo*

ONE MORNING, I discovered a book propping up a water pipe in the back stacks of the London Library, and was overcome by its true-life tale of love and survival.

The story of an illiterate American sailor, named Robert Adams, infatuated me. I vowed to base a novel on his *Narrative*, even if it was the last thing I ever managed to do.

My great fear was recounting a story that took place two hundred years before. I knew all about the period from reading accounts of the time but didn't have the guts to take the plunge.

So, although it was a circuitous route, I did what I'd done before.

I wrote a screenplay first, and used it as the framework.

In the run-up to knocking out the script, I wrote notes... thousands of pages of notes.

- Notes on Georgian London, where much of the action takes place.
- Notes on the depths of the Sahara.
- Notes on principal characters, and minor ones too.
- Notes on miscellaneous detail.
- Notes on the lens of my story and on the themes.
- Notes on history, fashions, and on points of etiquette.
- Notes on dozens of other things which were of no use in themselves, but which added to the overall taste, like a stock cube crushed into a stew.
- I even wrote notes on my notes.

There's no question I overdid it with the notes, but it

doesn't matter – because things happen when they are ready to happen… or, rather, when they're more than ready.

I once read a quote from Doris Lessing which helped me to understand how things are. I liked it so much I copied it out and taped it to the mirror in my bathroom so I'd see it first thing in the morning and last thing at night:

In the writing process, the more the story cooks, the better. The brain works for you even when you are at rest. I find dreams particularly useful… you can only learn to be a better writer by actually writing.

As a child I was slow to learn how to ride a bicycle because I feared falling off.

I kept the training wheels on my bike for ages, even though there was no need for them.

I just wanted to be safe.

One morning Greville, our storytelling carpenter, said he'd take me out. He promised that by the end of the afternoon I'd be riding without any help.

As I gazed on wide-eyed and fearful, he unscrewed the training wheels and ordered me to get on. I did as he said. On flat ground he pushed me as he held the back of my seat, while I pedalled super-fast.

At the far end of the driveway I braked, and cried out, 'Thanks for holding on!'

But Greville didn't reply.

Turning around, I saw he was way back in the distance.

I'd cycled fine without him or the training wheels.

My point is that I was ready to cycle by myself, even though I refused to believe it at the time.

Mentors are there to teach through their example, and there to give support by coaxing us on, even if they died centuries before we were born.

Although I'd researched and written *Timbuctoo* as a screenplay, I'd got into a big, sick, panicky state.

It was as though scaling the mountain was beyond me.

My wife had gone to India with the children to stay with her family for a few weeks, leaving me home alone. Moping around at Dar Khalifa, our home in Casablanca, I spent the days in my pyjamas, living on breakfast cereal, and the thin pickings found at the back of the fridge.

Except for the guardians and the housekeeper, the only people I ever met were the fresh crops of fans. Arriving regular as the tide, they'd all read my books on Morocco, and made a beeline from all corners of the earth.

I was ready for a change of scene.

One night I had an idea.

I'd fly up to London and write *Timbuctoo* on the very same desk at which Burton had supposedly translated his masterpiece, *The Arabian Nights*.

The circular desk was located in the library of The Athenaeum Club on London's Pall Mall.

Secret, sublime, and quite unsurpassed in its magnificence, the club was described by an American diplomat friend of mine as being 'right out of *Harry Potter*'. Membership of the Athenaeum was proof in Victorian society of having made it in life. Darwin, Dickens, Trollope, Thackeray, and Burton were all members. The club, founded in 1824, has boasted dozens of Nobel laureates, and all kinds of other luminaries from the sciences and the arts.

For much of his life my father was a member. He liked to work in the library – which is how I first got to hear of the fabled circular desk. When he died, I feared there would be no hope of ever reaching that seat of ultimate inspiration. But, fortuitously, and through an unlikely chain of circumstances, I was invited to join twenty years ago. The fact that lady members had recently been admitted made it all the more agreeable a place to be.

So it was that I found myself sitting where Burton had sat, my gaze roaming the glorious library shelves as his must have done a century and a half before me.

Flying up from Casablanca, I went straight from the airport to the club. Once there, I installed myself in the library, and began to write my historical novel, *Timbuctoo*.

For years I kept a note stuck to the wall above my desk.

A note to remind me of something very important:

DO WORK YOU ARE IN THE MOOD FOR!

It sounds obvious, but it isn't.

I'd often been coerced to toil away at something I was most definitely *not* in the mood for, a project which someone else wanted me to produce for their benefit, and their benefit alone.

If I've ever been put in the mood for something in the right way, it was sitting at the desk where Burton translated his *opus magnum*.

Without realizing it, I'd been ready to write *Timbuctoo* for months, just as I'd been able to ride the bicycle by myself without knowing.

As a result, the delivery was speedy, like a baby impatient to get out into the world. Having taken a room in the club's attic, I'd slip down into the library by seven each morning, and would write until midnight.

Within three weeks I had the first draft – all thanks to my mentor, Richard Francis Burton.

The editing process took far longer.

My fear was that I'd be crucified by the haughty literary set if there was a misplaced comma. So I hired six editors. Contradicting one another with their infernal suggestions, most of them meddled rather than edited. I'm used to having my work edited, but the process with *Timbuctoo* was different. For the first time I could decide which edits to use, and which to chuck firmly in the bin.

In the end I resorted to using the edits of the main editor, while culling occasional suggestions from the others. As the manuscript was chopped into shape – the shape I wanted – I gave thought to the book's physical form.

Were a publisher to have taken *Timbuctoo* on, they'd have probably released a standard hardback and then a mass-market paperback, and eBook editions a few months later. Relatively few people buy hardbacks these days, but publishers still tend to use the format – for two reasons.

They believe hardbacks offer certain gravitas, and claim the literary media will only review a book that's appeared in hardback form.

Generally speaking, the idea is outdated. It's true that, at one time, stuck-up literary editors at pretentious publications were equally stuck-up and pretentious about anything arriving in soft covers. Likewise, new books had a short window in which they would be featured in the print media.

But, as with everything else, the Internet changed all that.

Having been hidden away for weeks in what is surely the most elegant library in London, I felt justice had to be done.

*The Narrative of Robert Adams*, the book that had begun my obsession with the quest for Timbuctoo, had been published by my former publisher, John Murray, in 1816.

Bound in a magnificent quarto-size, it was set in a type called Bulmer, and had been printed around the corner from my seat at the round table in the Athenaeum Club. From the moment you open a copy of the *Narrative*, you can't help but be struck by the lavishness, and by an overriding sense that no expense was spared.

Although my decision would have caused consternation to a publisher's number-crunching department, the way forward was obvious to me...

*Timbuctoo* would have to be released in an edition fitting for the story it told.

To work out how best to envisage the right format, I closed my eyes, clenched both fists tight, and imagined myself as Sir Richard.

Not the two-dimensional man featured on the pages of

Wikipedia, or the one described in the scores of biographies. Nor the one you find by reading the books he left.

But the Burton you perceive only by studying the grouting between the tiles. Seemingly insignificant fragments that meant almost nothing alone. Yet, when collected altogether, they provided a dossier of overlooked information – the kind I'd need if *Timbuctoo* were to be the book worthy of the suffering of Robert Adams.

Sliding into Burton's body, exchanging my mind for his, I sensed the world open up in the most unpredictable and astonishing way. To think like the great Victorian polymath was to be freed from convention and restriction – and to live every moment as though it were a last hoorah.

Becoming Sir Richard – albeit in the limits of my imagination – the first thing to occur was that my jaw seized up. My teeth ground together, and I felt my features contort into a snarl. Not a snarl of anger, but one of profound no-nonsenseness.

Fists clenching all the more tightly, I saw the world – *my* world – through Burton's eyes, and I felt it in his bones.

Before I knew it, my focus had moved onto my novel *Timbuctoo*, and how best to release it. Until that moment I'd been fretting and flustering, anxious about overdoing it, or spending too much.

But all in an instant, the path forward became crystal clear. I would do what Sir Richard would have done.

That meant finding the best printer available, and sparing no expense.

Above all, though, it meant releasing the novel myself.

In a recent book I wrote about the prep school I was sent to as a child, and where I was torn to shreds almost every day for six years.

Rather than recounting the time with animosity, I described my gratitude – for the school's abhorrent regime enabled me to lose myself in imagination. I mention it here because of a comment in one of my form master's reports. He wrote: 'Tahir Shah would be a far better student if he were far less enthusiastic!'

I've often turned that line around in my head, doing my best to see how enthusiasm could be the curse with which that brutal wretch of a man considered me to be afflicted.

Enthusiasm has a lifeblood all of its own.

It's the reason Olympic athletes get up before dawn each morning, and push themselves to the limits. It's why explorers have endured the unendurable, and is the magic dust enabling creative people to keep going at all costs.

As I sat there in Sir Richard Burton's body and bones, my jaw clenched tight and my eyes narrowed with cold, slow disapproval – I was overcome with a sense of the great man's enthusiasm.

An unbridled zest for a project was what launched him and kept him on trajectory.

In any work I've ever done, I've harnessed the power of enthusiasm. Not in a wishy-washy way – but as though my life depended upon it.

Never have I raged with raw enthusiasm more abundantly than when I published *Timbuctoo*.

The first thing to do was to search for a printer to produce the finest edition of my novel imaginable, one worthy of Robert Adams and his tale.

What I had in mind was the kind of edition no commercial publisher would have allowed out of principle or because of expense. A thing of rare and unequalled wonder, it would be a book with embossed gold on the covers, marbled endpapers, a back pocket with curious inserts, the finest acid-free paper, bookmarks...

...and maps...

Numerous sheets of the most sublime and enormous maps.

Over weeks I corresponded with printers across Europe, the United States, and India. Hundreds of examples arrived by courier. While most fell far below Burton's exacting standards, one or two were fabulous.

But none were quite so tantalizing as the samples that reached me from a printer in Hong Kong. So impressed was I that, the day after his samples arrived, I boarded a flight to meet him.

When I set about restoring Dar Khalifa, our beloved home in the middle of a Casablanca shantytown, I learnt that the best craftsmen spoke very little at all.

Rather than deluge you with a torrent of self-praise, they'd sit there, sipping a glass of piping-hot sweet mint tea, lips tightly sealed. Whereas smug blustering types would rant on about their skill, a real *moualem*, a master, would allow his work to speak on his behalf.

The same was apparently true when it came to printers.

As subdued as he was precise, Maurice Kwan invited me into his office and listened rather than spoke. The owner of the impressively large Regal Printing Company, he might easily have palmed me off onto one of his many staff.

But he didn't.

Once I had outlined exactly what I wanted, Mr. Kwan scratched a thumbnail down his nose, blinking long and hard.

'We can do it,' he said.

'Yes, but don't you want to go over the details?'

Kwan blinked a second time – in the way a tabby cat might do. A blink of understated self-assuredness.

'We can do it,' he said a second time.

And he did.

Although, as I've said, no publisher in existence would have agreed to print my elaborate 'Burtonian' edition of *Timbuctoo*. Even if they had, as the author I wouldn't have been allowed anywhere near the production zone.

Working with Mr. Kwan and his team as I did, I felt like Alice slipping down the rabbit hole into a realm in which every detail was up for grabs.

For the first time in my professional life, I was invited to select the paper from swatches, the thickness of the boards, the ribbon for the bookmark, the structure of the pocket at the end, and dozens of other details.

*Timbuctoo* segues back and forth from Regency London to the parched wilds of the Sahara, in which the illiterate American sailor, Robert Adams, was enslaved for many years. As a lover of all things cartographic, I wanted to use maps contemporary to the era to give a sense of life in Georgian London.

By chance, I happened upon what is certainly one of the greatest works of cartography of the age – Richard Horwood's Plan of the English capital. Printed in thirty-two sheets at the end of the eighteenth century, the map features almost every building in existence at the time. Despite his expertise as a leading cartographer, the work was not a financial success – Horwood died in poverty.

Selecting six maps over which many of my novel's scenes were set, I sent them to Maurice Kwan and asked for them to be reproduced full size. I had expected him to protest at there being too many maps. But he didn't. Instead, he devised a system by which the maps would be folded intricately by hand, and then tipped into the book itself.

Inspired by Richard Burton and his 'Kama Shastra Society', I chose 'Secretum Mundi' as the name of my publishing firm. Meaning 'The Secret of the World', it was linked to the chain of transmission which had released Burton's own self-published masterpiece. More importantly, it was the foundation stone in a wall I hoped would help in redefining publishing.

When the first copy of *Timbuctoo* arrived by courier, I was staying in a small family-owned hotel on Mount Olympus. A thing of wonder, it was wrapped in sheets of ivory tissue paper, having travelled straight from Hong Kong. Weighing in at almost two kilos, it was monumental and absolutely perfect – all thanks to the soft-spoken Maurice Kwan.

The night the first copy reached me, I put it under my

pillow and said a prayer to Zeus, King of the Gods… After all, I was on Mount Olympus. I prayed circumstances would conspire to afford Robert Adams and his tale the publicity they deserved.

As so often happens in my life, my prayers were answered – but not for the reasons I may have wanted.

As the printed copies made their way westwards through Suez, I planned the media campaign. I hired a social media guru to get attention, had an elaborate website built, and wrote a slew of articles based on the story. And, inspired by *Masquerade*, the 1970s sensation by Kit Williams, I hid a gilded bronze head from the fabled city of gold in Timbuctoo, California. Yes, amazingly, there's another Timbuctoo. In fact, there are lots, with three of them at least in the United States.

But, alas, the treasure was never found.

Floods of messages came in from people who thought they'd cracked the clues running through the book. One adventurer who worked out the location put it all together from a thirty-second video I'd posted online. He'd managed to triangulate a range of details seen in the background. Triumphantly, he travelled to Timbuctoo with a shovel and GPS, only to find the designated spot had been dug up to build a new bridge. I often find myself wondering whether the contractors got their hands on the buried treasure, and what they made of it if they did.

Meanwhile, the printed copies of *Timbuctoo* finally arrived after their long voyage, and went on sale either side of the Atlantic. The hype had secured good publicity. But then, the day before the official launch, the prayers offered to Zeus on Mount Olympus were answered.

Under the flag of the so-called 'Islamic State', a Tuareg militia named Ansar Dine stormed into Timbuktu (to use the current German spelling), and began a reign of terror the likes of which the Dark Continent had not seen in centuries.

Schools and public buildings were torched, as were some ancient libraries of manuscripts from the Golden Age of Islam. Music, photography, and films were banned, women were ordered to be veiled top to toe in *burqas*, and anyone with a connection to the Occident was beheaded.

The morning of my launch, I woke to find the fabled city of gold, to which Robert Adams had been taken as a white slave two centuries before, on the front of every newspaper in the Western world.

I cursed myself for having prayed for publicity at any cost.

Horrified at what was happening at the hands of fanatical Islamists, I used the launch to draw attention to what was going on. In media terms, the publicity surpassed the wildest dreams of any publisher. I was featured on the leading TV and radio shows, published a lengthy article in *Newsweek*, and was the talk of the town.

Despite all the attention, my thoughts weren't on the book.

They'd moved on, and were searching for new material on which to feed.

From: *Timbuctoo*

# Trail of Feathers

LAST WEEK I was introduced to an elegant retired woman by a mutual friend.

The moment I set eyes upon her, I felt a pang of disdain, as though I despised her – in the same way that a cat gets spooked by something which makes no sense at all. My dislike wasn't based on how she looked, or what she was wearing, her perfume, or the way she had greeted me. Rather, it was founded on something far deeper, as though my inner radar was warding me away.

The meeting took place at the woman's home, a large, rambling mansion set among the most beautiful gardens imaginable. The house was filled with fine objects, each one of them more expensive than the last. We sat in the garden beneath a parasol, drinking iced tea. And for an hour or more we made polite conversation, discussing our lives.

As we chatted, I turned a question over in my mind.

Why was I being warned to despise her?

It made no sense, because I knew next to nothing about her. I have great respect for the gentleman who had introduced us, with whom I share very similar tastes.

Forty-five minutes into the conversation, I worked out the reason for my revulsion.

The woman hated travel.

I can't quite remember how the subject came up, but it did. Gushing on and on, like a river plunging over a waterfall, she railed at how people and places outside the area where she lived revolted her.

My life has always been about travel.

It's founded on a cornerstone of having the ground or the ocean beneath me, moving.

When I am still, I yearn to be moving – whether it be by bicycle, car, or truck, train, ship, aeroplane, or simply powered by my own legs.

Once moving, my brain works in an entirely different way to when I am stationary. Random ideas spark into being, join up with others, and I am suddenly catapulted forward, capable of intensely creative thought.

This alchemy occurs simply by movement.

My lust for travel has transported me to all kinds of places, and introduced me to people, magic, and the most indescribable wonders. From time to time I serve up slices of my journeys in book form, or for other types of media. But they are only ever the soup of the soup – a pale reflection of what really took place.

The journey that became *Trail of Feathers* was one of the most gruelling of my life. It introduced me to situations, the likes of which I had never imagined. It tested me, wooed me, wowed me and, most importantly of all, it changed me from the inside out.

In writing this book, I was charged with telling a story – bound by a contract with the publisher, Weidenfeld and Nicolson. As they continually reminded me, my duty was to summarize events in an amusing and intriguing way to please the book-buying public, them as the publisher and, lastly, myself.

Considering the book years later as I am doing, I am

amused at how the publisher had fought me every step of the way. They loathed the fact I wanted to include appendices – which they said were a 'waste of paper'. But their main gripe was that I'd announced I was leaving the firm. Enraged, they printed half the original number of copies and doubled the price. They only agreed to drop it when I noticed a little clause in the contract, obliging them to check the pricing with me in advance.

The book was the foundation for further journeys in Peru, which resulted in my travel book and documentary film, both titled *House of the Tiger King*. The most wonderful thing about a zigzagging journey like the one culminating in *Trail of Feathers* is that you don't have the power of hindsight. Rather, you're stumbling forward as a blank sheet of paper – with every situation and catastrophe shaping the steps ahead.

In my opinion, to be a great travel writer you have to be uninitiated, untravelled, and raw. Your eyes must see, your ears hear, and your nose smell – for the first time. If you're too seasoned, you don't have the intensity, the delight, and the full-spectrum experience. That's not to say the reflections of a travel-ripened wanderer can't have value, because they can. But the depth and range of the experience is quite different.

I often overhear people enthusing about the bucket lists of places to visit before they die. The same names are on there – Venice, Rio, Lhasa, the Arctic. Most of the time I roll my eyes and bite my lip. The last thing I want is to thrust my thinking down their throats.

The way I see travel, there's nothing so utterly sacred

as returning to the same place over and over through life. One of the joys of ageing is the ability to see the same thing differently, viewed through the lens of our own maturity.

To be honest, when returning to a place I have loved very deeply, or experienced love, I tend to be anxious and on edge. Nowhere and no one remains the same. Most of the time a place is changed as greatly as a traveller.

The reason for me explaining all this is that Peru is a country I have returned to again and again over the decades. I've seen it through the eyes of the uninitiated and through those of an older, more seasoned, adventurer. I've seen governments rise, promise the earth, and fall. Wealth get made and lost. Terrorists come and go. Tourism boom and bust.

Most of all though, I've seen myself reflected in the way I perceive the ancient Inca monuments, the plateaux of the Altiplano, the shoreline, desert, and the emerald-green expanse of the jungle. Every time I visit the country, I see it in a new way. But there's one thing which never changes…

My journeys through Peru always remind me what it is to be human. They remind me that, whomever I am at the time of my arrival and departure, I am no more than the most insignificant speck of inconsequence on a canvas of awe-inspiring wonder.

From: *Trail of Feathers*

## Travels With Myself

ONCE UPON A time there was a little boy who loved picking up pebbles on the beach.

No journey was complete until he'd spent time selecting the very choicest pebble, and stuffed it in his pocket. As soon as he got home, he put the pebble on his bedroom window ledge.

Some of the pebbles in the collection were smooth, cool and black, others were jade-green, more still were coarse, and yet more seemed to smell of a secret island far away.

As the years passed, the little boy took comfort in his pebble collection. In times of sadness they were there for him, a reminder of happier days – triggering memories of a beach, of rolling waves, or of the setting sun.

Time passed, and the little boy grew up.

It was time to leave home. He longed to leave on a journey in search of the Mango Rains. But, before setting out, he packed up all his belongings in tea crates and put most of them into a storage locker, beginning an eternity of waiting for things he once had loved.

Before clearing his bedroom, he shuffled over to the pebble shelf, stroked a hand over one or two of the stones, breathed in deeply. Then, taking a battered old shoebox from under his bed, he laid out the collection in nests of crumpled newspaper.

Twenty years passed.

The box was never opened, not once. The little boy, now a man, kept it locked up in a cupboard. He never forgot it was there, and would take comfort that it was with him.

The pebbles had been chosen at random over so many years, selected then studied, turned into the light, and observed from every angle once again. As the years passed, the types of stones he chose differed depending on his mood or age, the latter ones being quite different from the first one of all.

The stories in this book are like the pebbles in the little boy's collection. They're all different shapes and styles, and come from all corners of the world. Some will satisfy the curiosity of a select few, while others will appeal to all. I hope that the words will remind you of encounters you have had yourself, and stimulate thoughts you have never entertained before.

The common thread, if there is one, is fascination.

I've written about people, places, and things that have had a genuine and even mesmerizing grip over me. Whether they be the women on America's death row, or the thousands who live in Cairo's cemeteries, or portraits of lands through which my feet have strayed.

For me, this is a collection of work epitomizing travel through many realms – north, south, east and west. Each story is a fragment of a journey, a memory of happiness or hardship. Designed to be opened at random, this book will, I hope, be a companion on a journey, or in an idle moment at home. Although in random order, the styles and the quality of the writing vary – a reflection of my own journey on the writer's path.

The collection is a kaleidoscope of adventure, a lens

held over humanity and oddity, and the ordinary as well. In my professional life, I have striven to set down certain experiences in ink. My focus has always been on others, and their own human journey. But, reflecting on the people and situations I've encountered, as I am doing now, I see they have shaped me.

Of course they have.

Every journey, meeting, conversation, overheard truth or lie, has had an effect on the route I've taken, and the ultimate destination. Most of the time we like to think our destiny is shaped by overt decisions we've made. Nothing could be further from the truth. The course of our lives is fashioned by degrees of subtlety, and by the spaces between the words.

Half my life ago, I got chatting with a Samburu tribesman on Kenya's equator. He'd watched me take pictures of that exact spot, and asked what I was doing.

'It's the middle of the Earth,' I told him eagerly.

'Is it?'

'Yes!'

'Is that good?'

I frowned.

'Yes! It's so cool... and I'm standing right on it!'

'On what?'

'On the equator... the red line going round the middle of every globe.'

The Samburu gazed out towards the horizon, his cattle peppered over the landscape.

'I don't see a red line,' he said.

'Of course not. You see, it's not actually there.'

'So why are you caring about it?'

'Because,' I said, 'someone has to continue the tradition.'

'What tradition?'

'The tradition of being so foolish and so blinkered that I have no choice but to care.'

As for the little boy and his precious collection of pebbles, he's now living in Casablanca, and has a little boy of his own.

Yesterday I took him down to the beach just before dusk. Together, we watched the sun slip down into the calm waters of the Atlantic. When it was gone, we stood there in the twilight in silence. After a long while he asked:

'Shall we go home, Baba?'

I tapped a hand down to the beach.

'Pick up a pebble,' I said.

'Why?'

'Because it's time you started a collection of your own.'

From: *Travels With Myself*

# Travels With Nasrudin

THE WISE FOOL of Oriental folklore, Nasrudin is indigenous to a vast swathe of the globe – from Morocco in the west, to Indonesia in the east.

Appearing under different names, and in all manner of guises, he's universally admired – so much so that at least a dozen countries insist he was one of theirs.

Tales of Nasrudin's wise-foolery have been told in caravanserais and teahouses since ancient times, just as they are recounted today in cafés, office buildings, and homes the world over.

In the Land of Nasrudin, the wise are foolish and the foolish are wise.

Leading the listener through a keyhole into a realm that's back to front and inside out, the stories turn what we think we know and understand on its head.

At the same time, Nasrudin tales form a cornerstone in an ancient and advanced psychology. As one laughs at the off-beat humour, the subconscious turns the puzzle-joke around, working away at it like a child with a toy.

Nasrudin has been in my life since the day I was born.

He's travelled with me, chatted to me, laughed with me, and consoled me, while I've wandered the world, doing my best to make sense of it.

As the ground beneath my feet has passed, I've found myself considering familiar stories from the corpus of the wise fool in fresh ways. My journeys have been a key that opens a door to the Land of Nasrudin, just as the Land of

Nasrudin has been the key to my journeys.

In my life, as in my travels, humour is everything.

It's the way I deal with frustration, trauma, consternation, and pain. It's the lens through which I view uncertainty, too, and the mechanism I employ to push myself on and on to produce work, even when I'm a spent force.

For me, humour is a place of refuge, and of solitude... a magical dominion where I escape.

In that place I *am* Nasrudin, and he is me.

Everything in the realm of humour is turned on its head.

Red is blue, and blue is green.

Dogs are cats, and cats are dogs.

The moon is the sun, and the sun is the moon.

More importantly though, crises are solved with Zigzag Think – the kind characterized by Nasrudin. As a result of this, there's no war, famine, or social upheaval – because humour ensures harmony.

*Travels With Nasrudin* is a book that no one else could or would have written – not because it's better or worse than anything else, but because I've set it down as I experienced it – back to front and inside out – in the way I think the wise fool might himself have written it.

The life of a writer is one of contradictions.

We hide away in the Magic Zone as I'm doing now, and are expected to venture out from the shadows from time to time, to explain what we've published, and why.

I dread the limelight because giving reasons for my methodology makes no sense to me, in the same way that deconstructing a joke kills it.

In the safe refuge of my humour, 'Nasrudin situations' percolate up, like bubbles ascending from the ocean floor. Fragments of absurdity, they're delicious, satisfying, and abundant.

Just caught one as I wrote that last line. Here it is:

Nasrudin had secured himself the position as Professor of Humour at Samarkand University. He had been given the job and the professorial robe, as he was the only candidate. Day after day he gave terribly tedious lectures on the psychology of humour – explaining how comedy worked in monotonous detail.

One afternoon, a conceited student put up his hand, and said:

'I signed up for this course because I thought it would be easy, and that's the last thing it is.'

The wise fool regarded the pupil long and hard, and answered:

'Well, it seems that we are both disappointed! I signed up for this job because I thought the robe would make me seem taller, but so far there's been no hint of that!'

Sitting here as I ponder my associations with Nasrudin, and of the way he's impacted me on adventures – north, south, east, and west – I'm reminded of something central to the way I perceive the world:

Humour surely developed, not as a mere source of amusement, but as a teaching mechanism of its own.

Think about it.

All traditions use humour to present complex ideas, just as they employ stories to package the most important concepts imaginable. The way I see it, packaging ideas with a carapace of humour is rather like the stone of a plum being concealed in a delicious layer of flesh.

I was reflecting on this subject one afternoon with a former flower-child and fellow adventurer, in the backstreets of Kathmandu. Like me, she was a life-long admirer of Nasrudin, and had taken the so-called Hippy Trail overland from London in the sixties, having read my father's books devoted to the wise fool.

The woman, who never gave me her name, was English, although decades in the Nepalese capital had knocked her accent about.

'Nasrudin is more about what he is than what he isn't,' she said. 'He's the darkness behind the light.'

It seemed that my fellow traveller was fluent in the language of hippy-speak.

'He's the mouth-watering flesh that surrounds the plum's stone,' I added, hoping to speak the language, too.

'Nasrudin *is* the human experience,' the woman said.

'I wonder what he'd make of us sitting on this rooftop café, talking about him.'

The flower-child sighed.

'He'd think we're a pair of fruit loops,' she said.

From: *Travels With Nasrudin*

# BIBLIOGRAPHY

*Unless otherwise stated, all publications listed are by Tahir Shah*

A Moroccan Voyage, by Eric Mannaerts
A Son of a Son
Africa: The Anthologies
Beyond the Devil's Teeth
Café Clock Cookbook, by Tara Stevens
Casablanca Blues: The Screenplay
Ceremony: The Anthologies
Childhood: The Anthologies
City: The Anthologies
Confluence, by Laura Hudson Mackay
Danger: The Anthologies
Document Journal, by Vincent van Wijngaard
East: The Anthologies
Expedition: The Anthologies
Eye Spy
Frontier: The Anthologies
Hinterland: The Anthologies
House of the Tiger King
In Arabian Nights

In Search of King Solomon's Mines
India: The Anthologies
Journey Through Namibia
Jungle: The Anthologies
Legend of the Fire Spirits, by Robert Lebling
Marrakech: The Red City, An Anthology
Morocco: The Anthologies
Paris Syndrome
People: The Anthologies
Quest: The Anthologies
Scorpion Soup
Seven League Boots, by Richard Halliburton
Sorcerer's Apprentice
South: The Anthologies
Taboo: The Anthologies
The Caliph's House
The Flying Carpet, by Richard Halliburton
The Glorious Adventure, by Richard Halliburton
The Middle East Bedside Book
The Reason to Write
The Story of Morocco
The Travels of Ibn Battutah, by Tim Mackintosh-Smith
Timbuctoo
Trail of Feathers
Travels With Myself
Travels With Nasrudin

# A REQUEST

If you enjoyed this book, please review it on your favourite online retailer or review website.

**Reviews are an author's best friend.**

To stay in touch with Tahir Shah, and to hear about his upcoming releases before anyone else, please sign up for his mailing list:

✉ http://tahirshah.com/newsletter

And to follow him on social media, please go to any of the following links:

🐦 http://www.twitter.com/humanstew

📷 @tahirshah999

**f** http://www.facebook.com/TahirShahAuthor

▶ http://www.youtube.com/user/tahirshah999

**P** http://www.pinterest.com/tahirshah

**g** http://tahirshah.com/goodreads

# http://www.tahirshah.com

www.ingramcontent.com/pod-product-compliance
Lightning Source LLC
LaVergne TN
LVHW041248080426
835510LV00009B/640